Chakra Power Beads

Chakra Power Beads

Tapping

the Power of

Energy Stones

to Unlock Your

Inner Potential

Dr. Brenda Davies

Ulysses Press
Berkeley, California

Published by: Ulysses Press
P.O. Box 3440
Berkeley, CA 94703
www.ulyssespress.com

Library of Congress Catalog Card Number: 00-110577

ISBN: 1-56975-261-3

Printed in Canada by Transcontinental Printing

10 9 8 7 6 5 4 3 2 1

Editorial and production staff: Steven Zah Schwartz, Lily Chou,
    Marin Van Young, David Archer
Interior Design: Sarah Levin
Cover Design: Leslie Henriques, Sarah Levin

Distributed in the United States by Publishers Group West, in Canada by Raincoast Books, and in Great Britain and Europe by Airlift Book Company

This book has been written and published strictly for informational purposes, and in no way should be used as a substitute for consultation with health care professionals. You should not consider educational material herein to be the practice of medicine or to replace consultation with a physician or other medical practitioner. The author and publisher are providing you with information in this work so that you can have the knowledge and can choose, at your own risk, to act on that knowledge. The author and publisher also urge all readers to be aware of their health status and to consult health professionals before beginning any health program, including changes in dietary habits.

In loving memory of my mother, Hilda Todd

Acknowledgments

As always, a book does not come into being only by the love and labor of the author. The team that supports and cajoles is essential to the final delivery. The team on this occasion includes my editor, Steven Schwartz; my publicist, Sarah Fahey; Leslie Henriques, who designed the cover; Ray Riegert and all the other folk at Ulysses Press. Thank you all. Cindy, the librarian at Weimar Public Library, has been a great help and I have been supported throughout the whole project by friends too numerous to mention. One other person was extremely important: my mother, Hilda Todd, who sadly died before the book was completed. However, I have no doubt that she's watching lovingly and proudly on the arm of my father as she always did. Thank you to both, and to my children Keith and Lesda and daughter-in-law Elizabeth, who supported me through that difficult time. Last but not least, my friend Vickie, who has taught me so much—thank you.

Table of Contents

Introduction

For thousands of years, people in all parts of the world have used crystals and gemstones—not just as ornaments, but as powerful tools for tuning into our higher selves. It makes a lot of sense that many people are now discovering the power of gemstones and crystals. Not only are they beautiful, but they truly can help us relate to ourselves and each other better. It is wonderful to see so many people wearing chakra power beads—all the more reason to remember that these ancient pieces of the earth really *are* powerful, not merely fashion items.

Cultures all over the planet have, over many centuries, discovered profound ways of relating to ourselves and our divine nature. These practices, such as yoga, incorporate meditations and exercises designed to unify our entire being—body, mind, spirit, soul—all together, in deep connection with the universe. The chakra system, one of the most effective ways of getting in touch with ourselves, is not at all difficult for beginners to work with. Working with the chakra energy system is the perfect way to harmonize ourselves and get the most out of chakra power beads.

Learning more about your energy system, and in particular your chakras, will encourage you to make an informed choice about the stones you wear—not just to match your outfit, but to bring you health and well-being, calming or stimulating as necessary to bring you into harmony and balance. Each mineral has a variety of properties that can powerfully affect your health and well-being. Chosen with care, properly cleansed, protected, maintained and utilized wisely, they can powerfully influence every aspect of your life, from your general health to emotional issues such as coping with relationships; from helping unfold your innate talents and healing abilities to opening to your own divinity. For instance, fluorite can bring you mental clarity and assist learning; amber can calm you and bring a sense of peace; amethyst can help you sleep and turquoise can improve communication skills.

But more than this, each gemstone has an even greater impact when used with meditations and exercises that focus on a particular chakra. In this way, the healing can affect your whole life, unblocking your energy system, deepening your meditation, alleviating symptoms and healing illness. For example, citrine used specifically with your solar plexus chakra can help you realize your individual power and potential, increasing your motivation and drive and bringing prosperity into your life, while garnet used with your root chakra can help you develop a sense of belonging, improve your self-esteem and self-confidence and thereby disperse depression and the tendency to escape into addictive behaviors.

Working with crystals and gemstones should be light and joyful, since they have so much to offer and are beautiful to just have; however, I hope you will appreciate their power and wonder even more when you look at their history and find that in your hand you're holding something millions of years old that contains within it the essence of the planet. Whether you're just starting on your journey or are well on your way, whether you're a professional using healing techniques in your work or you're simply looking for a better way to live your life, it can be tremendously joyous and fulfilling to explore new perspectives, and I hope the exercises and meditations in *Chakra Power Beads* help in your exploration.

This book is arranged according to the seven centers of the chakra system. Chapter 1 deals with the energy system in general. (Later we'll be looking at what happens when for some reason the flow of energy gets stuck and what you can do about it. We're moving towards balance, so everything may need adjusting, even if just a little. Everyone, no matter how spiritually evolved, can benefit from a little fine-tuning!) In Chapter 2 we discuss gemstones in a general sense, including how to choose, cleanse, store and maintain them.

Each of the remaining chapters is devoted to a specific chakra—its functions and development and the problems that may ensue in adulthood if for any reason development has been arrested or delayed, or if there is physical damage (including damage from trauma or surgery) at the site of the chakra.

The qualities of the gemstones most appropriate for work with each chakra are described in detail, followed by an exercise, a quick tip and a meditation in each chapter to help you make a relationship with your chakra power beads or gemstones and to dedicate them for your use.

The two appendices at the end of the book give an overview of the historical use of gemstones and information about some interesting technical issues. If you want to learn more about your chakras, you will find a detailed account in *The 7 Healing Chakras* (Dr. Brenda Davies, Ulysses Press, 2000).

Whether you have some chakra power beads or gemstones and want to simply dip into one chapter to find out more about them, or you have some personal issues you want to deal with and decide to learn how to heal your whole energy system with the help of your gemstones, or you want a quick reference guide to bringing yourself better health and happiness, this book can help you. If you just want to have some fun finding out more about the bracelet you've been wearing, that's fine too. It is important to decide which stones are best for you and then make a relationship with them so they can serve you well and keep your energy as bright and pure as they are.

Nothing here is intended to replace any other help you're having. Please don't stop therapy or medication, or let something you find here interfere with anything else in your life, unless or until you want it to do so. However, as you handle your stones or chakra power beads with more knowledge of what they want to do for you, you may get a light, excited feeling as your soul responds to your approach and welcomes your awakening.

Your life can be full of the most amazingly wonderful things—love, joy and laughter—if you just reach out and have the courage to take them. Your journey can be exciting and adventurous, or peaceful and placid—the choice is yours. Even if thus far you have had a raw deal, don't despair—it can get better. And though having good friends and a supportive family is a blessing, in the end health and happiness are not dependent on anything external. Lead with your heart and you will eventually realize your own magnificence.

What You Will Need

Let's look at the things you'll need before you begin.

Sacred Space

In each meditation I'll suggest that you go to your sacred space—a peaceful place where you won't be disturbed. It might be outside sitting under a tree, or at the beach or in your own back yard, but I'm assuming you might want to do the work indoors at home. You can place in your sacred space some objects that are significant to you—for example, some candles (be careful when they are lit and don't leave them unattended), your books, a nice pen, some flowers or a plant, a vaporizer with your favorite oils. You'll find oils appropriate to each chakra described in *The 7 Healing Chakras*. If you don't have a room you can use, a little corner, or an armchair with a little side table will do. Even a box with a cloth over it can give you a feeling of a sacred space that is yours. Have a special cloth, or a cushion or a little altar upon which you can place your cleansed chakra power beads or gemstones before you dedicate them in the meditations. Though your stones, plant or flowers will keep the atmosphere clean to a great extent, singing bowls, bells and gongs and incense will help too.

A Notebook or Journal

You'll be using your journal at the end of each meditation, but use it also to keep a daily account of what happens when you embark on your healing journey with your chakra power beads and stones. I have no doubt that as you become more aware, you'll notice more of the synchronicities that the universe has always put in your path. Recording them gives life a new excitement—a bit like living your own detective story where you record the clues—but also helps keep an attitude of gratitude and childlike delight, blowing away any skepticism you may begin with. Another book for affirmations that you create along the way can be useful (your own affirmations are always best), but if you would like to have some affirmation cards to get you started you could order some from www.brendadavies-collection.com.

Some Recording Device

It can be helpful to record the meditations or have a friend read them to you. (Maybe you could then do the same for her). In either case, make sure you leave enough space and time to complete each stage before you move on. I'm sure you can intuit where you need to pause a little longer. But in any case, you can have your tape player close by, and you need hardly be disturbed by switching it on or off if necessary.

The Gemstones

Gemstones are so widely available now, both as chakra power beads and individual stones, that owning them doesn't have to be an expensive exercise. You will be drawn to what is right for you to begin with. You will find a section on choosing a bracelet or gemstone (or rather letting it choose you) in the next chapter, but if you really don't know where to start, you could begin with some clear quartz, which is the master healer suitable for every chakra; aventurine, which can similarly be used to balance everything; amethyst or rose quartz. Have fun buying them and observe what happens to your energy level, especially if you've prepared yourself by learning a bit about them and deciding what you need. (Be open to finding something you didn't plan to—on several occasions I've gone along with a particular stone in mind only to find that something else entirely almost jumps into my hand!)

Water

Always have a glass of water to drink at the end of exercises and meditations. Shifting energy from your cells is thirsty work! I use energized water, which I make by leaving a cleansed and energized quartz crystal in the jug of my water filter. Sometimes I also charge water with color by placing it in the appropriate colored bottle with the crystal whose energy I particularly want right now, leaving it in sunlight. This can be a powerful way to use gemstone energy. I would recommend that you use only rock crystal as a regular energizer for water to drink all the time. If you use any other gemstone, consider treating it as you would a good wine—have a small amount now and then (sometimes a few drops may be enough), perhaps daily over some time while you're working on a special issue. Better still, you could have a crystal therapist make you a special essence or elixir.

I hope you'll enjoy using *Chakra Power Beads*, have fun and also find yourself becoming more interested in healing yourself. This may be the start of a very special journey—I hope so. My heart and my love go out to you as you begin.

QUICK TIP

You can use crystal- or gemstone-energized water to bathe areas of your body that are giving you problems. Use only filtered water and don't apply to open wounds. If you have cancer it would be better to avoid water charged with rock crystal—you could choose something like amethyst instead.

How to Use Your Gemstones

Most stones are best when applied directly to your skin, though sometimes I like to wear them outside my clothes to catch the light and be cleansed and re-energized. Bracelets are ideal since they touch your skin and are generally in the light too. Sometimes I like to wear my stones as close as possible to the chakra I'm working on—I may have a single stone in a pocket where it's close to my sacral and root chakras, whereas necklaces and pendants will place them close to my throat or heart. Earrings are a good way to wear stones near your throat or brow chakra. I have been known to put a tiny, thin piece of stone in my socks to energize the chakras on the soles of my feet, since I often use my feet as well as my hands for healing. Sometimes gemstones need to be worn for a considerable time before anything seems to happen. Then we suddenly become aware, on looking back, that things have changed, though the movements were so subtle that we failed to see them at the time. This is why recording what you're doing in your journal is helpful, so you can refer to it later. Conversely, some stones may have a very quick effect, especially when there's imbalance or disturbance to clear up rather than when we want to effect some developmental change. Deciding what gemstones to wear might sometimes pose a problem. If you're working on a particular area or issue, just choose what is right for the appropriate chakra. If not, spend a moment looking at your gemstones or chakra power beads and you will suddenly know. I have my gemstone necklaces hanging on the corner of my dressing table mirror where they look beautiful, energize my bedroom and are also easy for me to choose from each day. They are so much more useful to you if you keep them where you can see them, and then you'll remember to wear them too.

Brenda Davies, M.D.
June 2001

ONE

The Energy System

Before we begin it would be good to clarify some of the concepts we'll be using in the following chapters. The energy of your chakra power beads or gemstones will work with your own energy to help clear up any difficulties you may have physically, emotionally or spiritually and will help you bring to the fore your innate talents and beauty. These stones are very powerful agents! But before talking about them, let's take a closer look at the energy system, spirituality and healing.

The Universal Energy Field

We exist in an ocean of energy, which we can refer to as the "universal energy field" (UEF)—sometimes simply "the field." In fact, we are part of this field. The atoms and molecules that make up our bodies are arranged in specific ways and vibrate at specific frequencies, making it appear that we are solid structures. The UEF changes in quality and intensity as it approaches us and it merges into our human energy field—our aura. The UEF is mainly space—as we are—but it contains light and sound waves, radio waves and also thought-forms and entities that you can learn more about if you're interested, when you're ready.

Your Aura

Your aura resembles an egg of energy surrounding you, in intimate contact with you, not dense enough to touch (as we usually understand touch). It affects and in turn is affected by every thought, word, feeling and memory you have. Most cultures have their own term for the life force—in Chinese medicine it's called *chi*, in India it's called *prana*, but everywhere it's the same force, the basic constituent of life.

This spiritual energy nurtures us. It's the stuff of our soul, helping us achieve more than our physical bodies possibly could otherwise, by contributing its qualities of clarity, courage, charity, endeavor, love, loyalty and faith.

The human body is generally so dense that we can see, touch, smell and feel it, though in fact, like everything else, it is an ever-moving mass of light—mostly space with perhaps five percent made up of atoms and molecules similar to those that form the rest of the universe. In good health, all of these molecules live in happy harmony, undergoing the millions of chemical reactions that make our bodies function so we can experience life as human beings. The dimension of our bodies most of us can't readily see is the etheric body (or more accurately, bodies), also known as the aura.

The aura is animated by swirling streams of energy created by its constantly moving chakras—vortices of energy at the interface of the physical and etheric bodies ensuring that the physical body is vitalized. This energy flow is as essential to our life and well-being as the energy we gain from food, water and air.

Each of the seven layers of the aura is associated with one of the major chakras. The first chakra corresponds with the layer closest to the physical body, the second to the next one, and so on. Each layer has a different color and function (though sometimes perceiving the separate layers is difficult and the whole appears like a shimmering mass).

Just as the physical body is in a state of constant change, with cells forever in a cycle of generation, decay and regeneration, so our aura is in constant movement. The chakras are to the aura what currents are to the ocean, transforming it into a living and tremendous force.

Not only does the aura transfer energy into and out of the physical body, it is also our greatest sensory organ. Before we meet someone physically, our aura meets theirs and an exchange of information occurs before we even speak. The aura holds essential information that fills the gap between the physical, psychological and spiritual, and between biology and mysticism.

The aura is also the repository of thought-forms and memory (though memory is also stored in every cell of our physical body). Thoughts and emotions are located in the aura as real substance, at times appearing like mucous, smoke or flashing light, passing between people as they interact. Unresolved energy such as unexpressed anger may stay in the aura or localized in the chakras for years. Healing and clearing blocks in these localities can have positive repercussions for every part of your system.

Can You See It, Feel It or Sense It?

For centuries, artists have depicted the aura around the heads and bodies of Christ and the saints, and mystics have talked of seeing the aura. Artifacts found in ancient archeological sites have the chakras clearly marked with colored stones. Within Jewish and Christian texts, Hindu Vedic writings, Buddhism and Native American teaching, there are references to light emitting from the body. Though generally the aura is invisible to most people, these examples remind us that some people are able to see it. Many children have the capacity to see the aura and even the individual chakras within it, but they usually lose this ability at an early age unless it's nurtured. Over the last 30 years it has become possible to photograph the aura and to quantify it electrically and electromagnetically, validating the claims of mystics and healers over the centuries.

The fact that most people can't see the aura makes it no less real. Wind, electricity and radio waves are invisible to the human eye, yet few people would deny their existence. Think of yourself like a peach with a stone in the middle and flesh on the outside—your body is equivalent to the stone and your aura the flesh. Though most people can't see the part around the outside, almost anyone can learn to see it; sensing it by means other than sight is often easier.

Even if you dispute the existence of the aura, you may admit to feeling a presence around some people. Powerful healers or mystics appear to have a sense of peace and even a tangible forcefield that surrounds them. Their powerful and highly developed aura makes it difficult to miss.

Likewise, from time to time you may have encountered someone who makes you feel uncomfortable for no apparent reason. This may be a consequence of their disturbed aura—perhaps because of pain, emotional scars and negativity they carry. And just as a highly evolved person can heal others by emanating healing energy, so those who are disturbed can unwittingly affect us.

Illness, age and gender can influence how the aura appears. Damage can also be recognized—seen by some people and felt by others. Sometimes tears in the aura are caused by surgery or trauma. Substance abuse—cocaine use, for example—can open holes in the aura that cause physical, emotional, mental and spiritual difficulties.

Skilled healers can look at an aura and use its appearance and the quality of its vibration as a diagnostic tool. Such persons can help us clean up our aura, providing a fresher and happier outlook than we've had previously. On our own, each of us can make our aura bright and shiny by clearing whatever clogs the flow of energy within it.

The Chakra System

The location and color of each of the seven major chakras will be described in detail in a chapter dedicated to it; for now it's useful to look at the system as a whole. Although in this book and elsewhere we look at each chakra individually, keep in mind that when discussing their role in our total functioning as human beings it's impractical to think of them in isolation—they are intimately connected and interdependent with each other.

There are seven major chakras, 21 minor and many lesser ones, the latter appearing over most of the joints and acupuncture points. Others are being revealed all the time. The minor chakras I'll be mentioning are in the palms of the hands and the soles of the feet.

Chakras appear like spinning wheels of light, and since they spin at different speeds, each emits a different light frequency, perceived as a different color. The lowest or base (root) chakra is red; the others bear the other colors of the spectrum—orange, yellow, green, blue, indigo or purple, and white. They are numbered one to seven starting at the base and moving upward to the crown. The major chakras have been given different names by different schools, which can be confusing—the names may be associated with location, or in some cases with function. For the purposes of this book, the seven chakras we'll focus on are called

Chakra 1—Base or root

Chakra 2—Sacral

Chakra 3—Solar plexus

Chakra 4—Heart

Chakra 5—Throat

Chakra 6—Brow

Chakra 7—Crown

All of the major chakras can be seen or felt at both the back and front of the body and are connected centrally. Ideally there should be a free flow of energy from front to back and back to front. The crown and base form a vertical axis, which runs through the center of all the other chakras. This vertical power channel or current can be felt above the head, and forms a funnel of energy extending down from the base of the spine between the legs toward the ground. Energy flows in both directions, the root chakra taking in energy from the earth and the crown chakra bringing in energy from above. The root lets us ground energy the way a lightning rod grounds electricity; the crown chakra forms our direct access point for higher spiritual energy.

The minor chakras are found at the front of each ear, above each breast, in the palm of each hand and the sole of each foot, behind each eye, over the ovaries and testicles, and behind each knee. There are also ones connected to the stomach, the thymus, below the throat chakra (between the collar bones) and at the major solar plexus chakra; two are situated at the spleen and one near the sacral chakra.

The chakras penetrate both the aura and the physical body, energizing and vitalizing us on all levels and affecting every system—metabolic, glandular, immune, nervous, circulatory, respiratory, digestive, reproductive, musculoskeletal, etc. The health of our chakras determines physical, emotional and spiritual development and, in turn, other factors in our development influence the health of the chakras.

All of the chakras are present in a rudimentary form at birth. As with the rest of our body, early trauma, whether physical or emotional, can arrest, distort or otherwise mar their development.

As the chakras draw in energy from the universal energy field they continually revitalize our whole being. Though we can survive with an energy system that's clogged up, a reduced energy flow diminishes our sparkle, joy and total well-being. Healing cleanses and re-balances the chakras, releasing old energy, relieving stagnation and restoring harmony, encouraging free energy flow and promoting our innate healing powers.

Blocks in the System

Since the aura and the chakras within it are simply extensions of your body, just as you can tell your arm to lift up and it does so, you can tell your chakras to open or close and in good health they will. After a while they'll do so simply with a thought, and eventually without even the smallest cognitive step. Note, however, that though your arm will move at your command, sometimes it will jerk reflexively, for instance if you touch something hot. Your chakras act in the same way. Reacting to some perceived harm or to a memory—physical, emotional or spiritual—they may either open wide or snap shut. And just as you may have some injury that would prevent you from lifting your arm, sometimes your chakras are unable to work because of something that has happened either to harm them or to prevent their development. Because generally you can neither see nor feel them, damage might continue for years without notice while the effects drag down your health or your ability to enjoy your life. Healing and retraining the chakras will give you choice and control.

When a chakra is not functioning well, we often say it's blocked, though in fact it might be brittle and stuck wide open—as is often the case in the heart chakra; or it might be too active, or spinning too slowly or hardly at all, or turning in the wrong direction, or out of balance. When the chakras are "open" (though they are rarely completely closed), there's little choice but to deal with the energy flowing through them. Although it's true that in general the more energy flow there is, the healthier we are, sometimes we've learned to close down our system because we're not ready to deal with the psychological or emotional pain the energy brings as it makes us face issues we'd prefer not to. Since all of the chakras are in intimate communication, each is affected by the functioning of the others, and if one is closed down there tends to be a domino effect in the others.

Each of the major chakras is also associated with a major gland of the endocrine system and its dysfunction will therefore have far-reaching physical effects. For example, since the throat chakra is associated with the thyroid gland and the thyroid gland affects growth, motion, temperature control and much more, damage to the fifth chakra may hinder any of these functions.

All of us resort to blocks at times to regulate the flow of energy, depending on what we feel we can cope with at the moment. Sometimes these temporary blocks can be useful for avoiding unwanted energy from other people. Mostly we do this unconsciously through body language, where we may cross our legs to protect our base and sacral chakras, or cross our arms to protect our heart and solar plexus, or put our heads in our hands to protect our throat, brow and crown.

Since blocks can become fixed or habitual ways of damming the flow and avoiding certain aspects of ourselves, it's worth exploring ways to clear them when we're ready. They may have become outdated and are now simply impeding growth. All can be cleared and healed with time, gentleness and a genuine desire to do so. Clearing blocks is like a spring-cleaning exercise that allows a breath of fresh air—in this case spiritual energy—to flow through. Clear, fast-spinning chakras are essential for nurturing and revitalizing the physical body, and to ensure emotional, psychological and spiritual health. However, you and only you have the right to decide if and when you want to dismantle any blocks you may have. Don't let anyone attempt to do it for you unless you trust them completely and have invited them to assist you with healing or therapy.

Don't be alarmed or discouraged if you clear up one area only to turn around and find that it's blocked again. If you've been living a long time with only a paucity of energy, you may at first find it difficult to live with absolute clarity. Sometimes a strong flow of clear sparkling energy is a very rich diet to cope with! Healing will only occur to the extent that you can deal with it. Miracles do occur, but not everyone is ready for one. After all, your current state of health and well-being is what you're used to, even if you don't like it much. Also, you're still learning something from being there. Changes may need to occur gradually—sometimes it's terrifying to let go of what you know and leap into the void! Be gentle and compassionate with yourself.

The Soul

The soul has been variously defined as the part of us that's essential to life and yet has no tangible or visible substance; as the immortal essence of our being; as our higher self; and as the dimension of us that incorporates our functions of loving, thinking and volition. It is responsible for lifting us above the human and into the divine, to our spirituality. Some would say it's the aspect of God that resides in us and joins us as a single body of humanity. You can find a greater discussion on this in *Unlocking the Heart Chakra*.

Spirituality

Spirituality actually has little to do with religion, though it's often in religion that those in pain or distress seek it. While being a personal expression of who we are, spirituality nevertheless unites us, whereas, sadly, religion is often divisive, separating us into sects, spreading suspicion and mistrust. Whatever words you use to describe the phenomenon of spirit, you can learn to be consciously aware of this aspect of yourself and to start using it as a powerful tool that will make astounding changes to your life. We're all spiritual beings, with our spirituality an ever-present, if unacknowledged, factor in our daily lives. If it's a dimension of yourself you haven't started to use, working with gemstones will help you not only to recognize your spirit, but to mobilize it and let it participate it in every aspect of your life as you become healed, whole and healthy.

Healing

Healing means making whole. It helps return what is unhealthy, diseased, unbalanced, compromised or unwell to its natural state of health and well-being; it helps growth and development where these are needed. In whatever form it takes, healing always empowers, encouraging our consciousness to take responsibility for the well-being of the whole. It helps us dislodge some of the debris that has clung to us during our experience of life thus far and open up new areas to help us have a happy, healthy and fulfilled life. Old feelings, hurts and bitterness that have clogged our natural flow and cut us off from the love that nurtures us can be finally let go.

Some areas may have lagged behind with their development, whether because of pain that was going on when they would normally have been developing, because of blocks at other areas of the energy system, or because of some trauma to the physical site where the physical body and the spiritual body intersect. Surgery can leave holes in the aura and can also cause some distortion of the chakras themselves; they then need healing to restore natural energy flow.

Whatever the illness, many studies have proven that the psychological state of the person is of prime importance in the process of recovery. And since our psychological state is dependent on our peace of mind, which in turn is a function of our spirit, recovery from illness always involves a spiritual process. Essentially, the body cannot heal until it comes into balance with the mind and the spirit, nor can healing occur in the absence of love.

Acts of spiritual healing are reported in both the Old and New Testaments of the Bible as well as in other ancient and religious writings; yet they're not simply a thing of the past. In the twenty-first century, healings still take place all over the world every day—in churches, synagogues, mosques and other holy places, in doctors' clinics and operating rooms, by the roadside at accidents and in many other places. The mother who holds her sick baby and allows her love to flow into the child is aiding its recovery even though medical help may also be required. There are doctors who pray for their patients, and surgeons who pray before going into the operating room. There are those who work specifically as spiritual healers in their own homes and in practices around the world. In every culture, there are shamans who ask for divine intervention for themselves and others. In fact, healing occurs wherever we have the love and faith to call to some power of goodness beyond ourselves for help.

There are numerous tools we can use for healing; gemstones are a convenient and potentially effective one. They are more than willing to give us their energy, to protect us, to help absorb negativity from around us and as it arises when we feel depressed, and to bring our energy into balance.

Absent Healing

We do not have to be present to receive healing or effect healing; distant or absent healing is a powerful tool used by many healers today. Most of us work with a list of people who have asked for healing and spend some time each day focusing loving, healing energy toward them and also toward troubled areas in the world. Some individuals who strongly object to the concept of healing do not wish to receive, and it's essential to respect this wish. Sending out healing to those who don't want it is a form of assault and must be avoided. To send out love to the planet with pure heart and our highest integrity, with the intention that this will go to heal wherever it's needed most, is a different matter, however, and I know that the healing is then directed by a higher wisdom.

Self-healing

The love and energy we use to heal others can also be used to help heal ourselves, though sometimes we do need someone or something external as well, whether a doctor or other practitioner, medication or practical help. You have the power to clear your energy, access your spirituality and mobilize your innate ability to heal yourself, which aids you and anyone who is trying to help you. Using crystals and gemstones as part of that healing adds another dimension as you take responsibility for your own well-being.

Getting really well can be fun. You will get there at your own pace. Sometimes progress is rapid—things can happen quickly when you make a conscious decision to move on. However, sometimes we need to allow our bodies, minds and souls to adjust gently as we grow into a new way of being. Whichever way you choose, I hope it will be light and loving.

CLOSING DOWN

At the end of each meditation it would be wise for you to close down your chakras before you go off again into your daily life, where you may be bombarded by other people's energy. The chakras will quickly adjust themselves to the position you find most comfortable and which is safe.

A quick and efficient way to close down is to start at the crown chakra and imagine a white flower; let it close its petals. Then move down the chakra system, imagining a deep blue flower for the brow chakra, a blue or turquoise flower for the throat, a green flower for the heart. Visualize a yellow flower at the solar plexus and an orange one at the sacral chakra, allowing their petals to close too. However, the red flower you visualize at your root chakra stays open to keep you grounded. With a single thought you can then surround yourself with white light and you'll be fine.

TWO

Getting to Know the Power of Your Gemstones

Knowing more about your gemstones will help you develop a good relationship with them. In this chapter we look at what gemstones are, how they were formed and how they have been viewed over the ages. We also look at how you can choose stones for yourself, and how to clean, store and maintain them. The chapters that follow will help you dedicate and attune to your stones as we study the chakras and the gemstones relevant to them. As you read this chapter, try to hold in your mind any stones or beads you may possess, and feel the history of these pieces of the earth and all they have experienced before they came to you.

So . . . What Are Crystals or Gemstones?

Though we often refer to gemstones as crystals, for some of them this term is geologically incorrect. Most do have a crystalline structure, but some are rocks and others, such as amber, jet, coral and pearl, are organic materials (from plant or animal sources). To cover them all, I will use the terms stones or gemstones in the text. The word crystal comes from the Greek *krustallos*, meaning ice, since originally people thought clear quartz—rock crystal—was formed by the freezing of a mineral solution, a view that remained until the eighteenth century. Crystals are perfect geometric forms that develop in one of seven different characteristic patterns (which you can read about in Appendix 2). Examining the perfect and unique structure of a stone can help determine whether it is natural or synthetic. Synthetic stones may have great beauty, color and brilliance, but they do not have the power of real gemstones.

There are probably 50 or more commonly used natural gemstones, prized for their beauty and healing properties; some of course, such as rubies, sapphires, diamonds, emeralds and natural pearls, are precious also because of their comparative rarity and durability. Even so, their healing properties render all gemstones more valuable than their monetary worth. Cutting and polishing enhances the stones; it allows light to enter them and be refracted (bent) and reflected, making them ideal for use as jewelry. Those that are technically crystals have a characteristic inner lattice of molecules that remains the same no matter how the stone is cut, ground or broken. Though the outer shape of the stone may vary depending on the forces present when it developed, the angles between the faces are always similar for each particular gemstone. Even when tumbled, the inner structure and the minute angles of the surface are not lost. In fact, each crystal is composed of many smaller units, all of similar structure and shape.

Though most gemstones can be found in several different colors depending on the temperature at which they formed and the minerals in the vicinity, we often associate them with a particular color.

Inclusions

Inclusions are substances that may have become trapped inside as the gemstone developed, or entered later through cracks. These may be plant or animal matter such as pieces of moss or insects, or bubbles of gas or liquid, or indeed other crystals or pieces of mineral from the site where the stone developed. Sometimes one crystal develops on top of another, giving it a special beauty, with either a phantom or a rainbow effect inside. Inclusions may help pinpoint exactly where a gem came from, often very accurately and specifically, even to the particular mine, and are therefore important in defining a particular stone (useful for insurance purposes in the case of extremely precious stones). They may also increase the value of the stone—for instance, amber is more highly prized when it has insects millions of years old trapped inside it, and clear quartz with rutile inclusions (commonly known as rutilated quartz) is sought after. Though inclusions are often visible to the naked eye, they can sometimes only be detected by careful examination.

How the Gemstones Formed

The gemstones we now use have an ancient history. Understanding it can add to the bond we form with these beautiful pieces of the earth. About 4.5 billion years ago, our planet was simply a white-hot ball of gas that gradually cooled, and as it did so, lighter minerals rose to the surface and heavier ones such as iron and nickel sank. The inner core of the planet remains molten today, and around it the mantle, a hot fluid layer made up of various minerals, is constantly moving under the outer crust—the part we live on. Some crystals are millions of years old, and took thousands of years to develop. Others may have been formed in an instant as gases cooled upon reaching the surface of the earth.

Most gemstones are composed of minerals found in rock either on the surface or deeper. Quartz (silicon dioxide) is the most common rock found on the earth's surface and, as sand, covers much of the planet. This quartz often bears stains of soluble iron, which gives sand its characteristic color. (The good feeling we get while walking on the beach is not only from the negative ions of the ocean spray but also because we are walking on quartz!). Many other gemstones are made from silicon dioxide as well, though colored by other elements.

Gemstones are usually composites of the gases, liquids and solids of the earth and the process that formed them has a bearing on their structure, their clarity and their ability to store and radiate light and electromagnetic energy. Generally speaking, the more purified the matter they formed from, the more brilliant their color and clarity. However, it is not their beauty that causes them to be powerful. Sometimes rough, unpolished chunks—for example, natural pieces of unpolished rose quartz—have strong healing properties. And size makes a difference—

most gemstones are so minute that it is impractical to use them as healing stones.

Types and Properties of Gemstones

Magmatic or igneous crystals—The layer of magma, or molten rock below the earth's crust, is only revealed when a volcano erupts. The lava, molten material and burning gases from the earth's interior, cools and solidifies, forming igneous gemstones. An example of igneous crystal is quartz in its several forms—clear, amethyst, citrine and rose quartz, among others.

In healing, igneous stones tend to encourage learning processes—thought, behavior and spiritual growth. In situations where we need rapid growth or learning, where there are new challenges and beginnings, the igneous crystals are a good choice.

Sedimentary—Sedimentary stones are formed when solutions of minerals solidify on or near the earth's surface. Examples are calcite, agate and rhodochrosite, stalagmites and stalactites.

In healing, sedimentary stones can help us with situations that have arisen because of factors external to us—in our environment, our homes and workplaces—and also within the relationships that are the substance of our lives. Stones from this group will generally help us resolve situations that have hurt us and made us alter our course, preventing us from enjoying our lives in the present by staying with us and causing

---

QUARTZ

Quartz is a generic term for a number of stones that have a similar hardness, structure and chemical composition. The colors vary according to the different minerals found in the area where the stones formed, and according to the temperature prevalent at the time of their formation. The group includes amethyst, citrine, rose quartz, smoky quartz, tiger's eye, cat's eye and hawk's eye, as well as clear quartz, or rock crystal.

---

inner conflict. Symptoms such as stress, anxiety and tension that have resulted from such inner conflict can be soothed and harmony restored.

Metamorphic crystals—Metamorphic stones are formed where already existing crystals undergo chemical and structural changes because of the pressure and high temperature in the lower regions of the earth's crust. The atoms reorganize to form a "new" stone. Examples of metamorphic stones are garnet, which comes from shale, and marble, from limestone. In healing, these sorts of stone help us look at anything in our lives that is outgrown, outdated and needs to be changed. In using them, often we find that we become dissatisfied with certain aspects of our lives and are suddenly able to let go of the old and embrace the new, to close one chapter in our lives and begin another. Thus these stones help us define our direction and purpose and transform our lives.

Condensed and solidified vapors—These crystals form from gases and vapors that escape and cool in vents in volcanic areas. An example is sulfur.

The Present

Various properties of gemstones make them useful in the modern world. Rubies are used in lasers; quartz crystals are found in watches, ultrasound, electronic equipment and computers, earphones, oscillators and condensers; diamonds are used in grinding equipment and drills; tourmaline develops an electric charge when heated or under stress and is useful for thermometers and for detecting depth and pressure under water; quartz forms an electric charge on its surface when under mechanical stress (a characteristic known as piezoelectricity) and is therefore ideal for use in gas lighters and pick-ups for electronic sound amplifiers. And where would we be without the silicon microchip?

Gemstones can transmit, receive, reflect and store light and electromagnetic energy. It is not only their beauty that has led them to be used to adorn the crowns of kings and queens, add their protection and blessings to swords and armor, or be used as jewelry throughout the ages. They also have mystical and healing properties they've been revered for in many cultures down the centuries, at least from the time of the ancient Sumerians and Egyptians. They can help us develop our intuition, raise our consciousness, improve our mental clarity, change and stabilize our moods, lift our spirits and bring us toward harmony and health. If we wish to experience these benefits, though, we must use them consciously and ethically, for their power is greater than we may imagine, and if used unwisely they can hurt as well as heal.

How Do We Use Gemstones for Healing?

Properly used, gemstones can support, strengthen and restructure the chakra system and cleanse the aura as they resonate with our natural frequencies. Not only can they open or close, expand or contract the chakras, relieve congestion and remove old energy debris, but they can actually help rebuild torn and damaged chakras. Strengthening the junction between the physical body and the spiritual body, they can also help us be more receptive to healing.

Stones may be placed directly on the chakras, at other places on the body to support the chakras, over injuries such as strains and sprains or within folds of bandages (try a small piece of malachite between the layers of bandage around a sprained ankle), or around the body to encourage the flow of electromagnetic energy. Sometimes they are made into gem essences and elixirs that are then swallowed, though these can be very potent and should be made with care by a crystal healer. Gemstones should not be placed directly on open wounds.

Sometimes gemstones are chosen for their specific qualities and sometimes for their color. You are intuitively aware of your healing needs and will usually pick exactly what you need if you take a moment to pause, reflect and let your intuition guide you.

Our body naturally contains silica, and therefore has a natural affinity to quartz. Quartz (silicon dioxide) can balance our electromagnetic energy. Quartz crystal holds the vibration of white light, which naturally refracts into the colors of the spectrum, acting directly on our chakras. (We discussed the energy system in more detail in Chapter 1—you can also refer to my book *The 7 Healing Chakras* for a broader description and discussion.)

In another example, the ruby emits exactly the same frequency as the healthy root chakra. If the root chakra is out of balance, the ruby can be used to restore it. Using stones for their color-balancing effect is a fairly long-term project and the stones need to be worn directly on the skin. Power bracelets are ideally suited to this sort of use.

Following is a rough guide to gemstones, arranged by color:

Black stones such as smoky quartz, black tourmaline, jet and obsidian tend to remove blockages, relieve pain and promote relaxation both physically and emotionally. As stress diminishes, resilience and the ability to cope increase.

Red stones such as ruby, garnet, spinel and jasper are stimulating both physically and emotionally—the deeper the red the more stimulating the effect. Yet they can also keep us grounded with an inner sense of security and calm. The heart can be stimulated and circulation improved. Digestion and absorption increase, and on a psychological level emotions are intensified and the capacity to persevere and endure is strengthened. Learning and spiritual growth quicken.

Pink stones such as rose quartz, pink tourmaline and rhodochrosite bring harmony, sympathy, empathy and compassion.

Orange stones such as carnelian, orange tourmaline and coral have a vitalizing effect on the sacral chakra, improving our sexual energy and sensitivity while stimulating creativity and improving our capacity to feel joy in our lives and live in harmony with others.

Yellow stones such as citrine, yellow calcite and tiger's eye stimulate the solar plexus and help us be cheerful and positive with a good attitude to life, a willingness to accept and use our power wisely, to live out our lives prosperously and to utilize our will wisely. They help us be sunny, self-confident and carefree with the knowledge that we are in charge of our lives.

Green stones such as aventurine, jade and malachite are cleansing and detoxifying, helping bring physical as well as emotional and spiritual harmony. For a while green stones may appear to cause emotional disharmony as painful emotions are allowed to surface before optimism, hope and inner peace arise.

Blue stones such as turquoise, blue lace agate and calcite are cooling, calming and balancing. Supporting the function of the throat chakra, they encourage openness, honesty and integrity as well as improved communication.

Violet and deep blue stones such as amethyst, lapis lazuli, sodalite and sugilite are useful when dealing with sorrow and at times of trauma. They also aid clarity and spiritual growth in general, allowing us to improve our spiritual vision and the gift of clairvoyance. Working on the brow chakra, they can also help us awaken our innate wisdom.

White and clear stones such as quartz, diamond and pearl help us become as clear and pure as they are, and can be used for any kind of healing (though clear quartz is not good where there is cancer, since it promotes the growth of cells). Spiritually they help us open to the highest possibilities of our divinity and balance our spiritual energy while at the same time keeping us grounded.

Sometimes crystals and gemstones are collected in "chakra sets" of seven colored stones to use for healing and balancing the chakra system. Their vibratory qualities can also come into play as sound, when rubbed or struck gently and when formed into bowls that emit vibrations to align and heal the chakras.

Stones may affect different people in different ways, and some stones are more powerful than others of the same type. Since all of them are powerful and even subtle movements within the aura can change the energy field, it is essential to understand their true nature, to cleanse and attune them and to use them responsibly; otherwise their power can work against us.

Choosing Your Gemstones

It has often been said that we do not choose crystals—they choose us. So in many ways you need not worry, because the right stones will come into your possession, and when they feel like they're yours, they'll stay with you until their work with you is complete. Should you "lose" them, they have chosen to do their work elsewhere. As you'll see from my story at the end of the chapter, sometimes they return quite strangely! Some of my stones have come as gifts (it is said that turquoise and jade should be given rather than bought), and some I have purchased. A Russian academic pressed one of my favorites, a lemon quartz, into my hand as I dropped him off at the airport on his return home. A piece of jade was bequeathed to me. A huge piece of celestite almost leapt into my arms in a shop in London some years ago and has accompanied me around the world ever since, despite the fact that it is very heavy. Your power bead bracelets will also choose you.

If you are buying an individual stone or a power bracelet, it's important to have in mind the purpose you intend it for. Stones you want for healing work might be different from those you buy for meditation or for beautifying your home and harmonizing energies there. A bracelet or necklace you intend to wear regularly for your own healing and protection will be different from something you intend to give away or simply wear to match an outfit. Healing stones must always be natural—synthetic stones, though they may be beautiful, don't have the energy of the earth.

Focus on the purpose you have in mind and be silent for a few moments to allow you and the stones to tune in to each other. Try bringing to mind an image of how you would like the stones to help you or the person you're buying them for. Then ask that the right stones be attracted to you, and you to them. If you are choosing from a collection in a store, you might find that as you look at them, one particular stone or bracelet seems to pull you to it despite the fact that it might look similar to the others. Ask to hold it and you will find that it feels comfortable in your hand and may even make the palm of your hand tingle or your heart suddenly feel loving. Sometimes you will need to choose by gently moving your hand, palm down, above the stones.

You may feel an urge to pick one up or find that your hand tingles as you pass over it. As before, pick it up and hold it and see if it feels right. If so, this is the one. When you have chosen it (or it has chosen you) be sure to express your gratitude and to treat it as a new and precious friend—which of course it is.

Cleaning Them

Now that you have your stones, it's important to cleanse them as soon as you can, and in so doing start to bond with them. Bear in mind that they have been hewn from the earth; often chemicals have been used in their preparation (solvents or even explosives), and other people have touched them and left their energy. The stones may have been in situations where they absorbed negative energy, and this must now be released. You are now the custodian of your stones and, unless you intend to use them for professional healing, the only energy they should hold now is yours or the vibrations they absorb in healing or protecting you.

How often you clean them depends on how often you use them or what they are used for. You'll soon be able to tell if they lose their sheen or become pale or sticky, and thereby know that cleaning is overdue. The crystals I wear when working I may clean every day, whereas those in my home I clean less often—but always if some negative energy has been released, for example in an argument. Depending on where I am in the world, I try to at least put them outside in salt water at the time

---

BE AWARE…

Wash your hands carefully after handling stones in shops and at fairs and other public places. Some of the stones bear a toxic chemical residue and some may contains substances that can be harmful to us. For instance, realgar contains arsenic, cinnabar contains mercury and malachite dust can cause lung, skin and eye irritations.

MY OWN EXPERIENCE—A SHOW OF LOYALTY!

There are many stories about how crystals will demonstrate their loyalty to us. Some years ago I returned late at night to my home in London from a workshop, with my beloved crystals in my suitcase. The following morning I was upset to find that my case had been stolen, and I spent several hours in meditation, communicating with my stones, telling them that wherever they were, I wanted them to do good, but that if they could return to me I would receive them lovingly. I then simply let go and knew that the right thing would happen. About three weeks later, when I was back in my home in Texas, a young man from the Czech Republic walked into my London office with my suitcase, having found it abandoned on the roadside about twenty miles away. All of its contents were there—including all the crystals, which were gleaming despite having worked so hard to get back to me. If nothing else, they seem to have conferred the wisdom on the thief that neither they nor the rest of my belongings were his, and that they should be returned to me. I've often wondered if he ever stole again!

of the full moon. Ideally no one should touch your stones but you, but often well-meaning people will pick them up to admire them, leaving their energy, which you may want to remove. Sometimes, however, you may want to ask some healer or spiritual teacher to hold your stones and bless them.

There are several ways to cleanse and revitalize your stones. Most importantly, do it when you are in a good frame of mind—though usually, no matter how you feel, starting to handle your crystals will usually lift your mood and you may find yourself briefly in a different, silent but energized world. With some exceptions (notably celestite, which is better smudged; halite, which dissolves in water; hematite and iron pyrites, which can stand only a brief wash), they tend to like water. Though you can hold them under running water or take them into the sea with you, I usually use a bowl of filtered water with a little sea salt and steep them for a few hours or overnight before rinsing them in pure water and then patting them dry before I use them again. Sometimes I add a few drops of cider vinegar, a drop of rosemary or grapefruit oil and/or some rescue remedy, and then soak them for only about ten minutes. Liz Simpson in her beautiful *Book of Crystal Healing* (Gaia Books, 1997) suggests also using crabapple flower essence. Sometimes I put them out in the rain.

For gemstones that don't like water, or if you're in a hurry, you can use other methods. After the initial cleansing to remove any toxic residue, you can clean your stones by simply holding them and asking that light be shined into them. (The meditation at the end of this chapter will show you how). Invariably they like light and it will revitalize them. I like to put mine in a sunny windowsill, to wear them on the outside of my clothing so they catch the light, to place candles around them and to put them out in the garden at the time of the full moon. I also use smudging—cleansing with the smoke from smoldering herbs, especially sage. Sometimes I revitalize them with sound with a singing bowl, gong or bells, sometimes place them in dry sea salt or on a large amethyst cluster, and sometimes I retire them for a while or completely by burying them in the earth. If I forget where I put them, I assume that the earth wanted them back!

Dedicating and Programming Gemstones and Power Beads

Crystals and stones should be utilized only for good—yours and everyone else's. So when you have cleaned your stones, having a ceremony to dedicate them is a good idea. At the end of each chapter you'll find a meditation that guides you to dedicate your stones and form a relationship with them before wearing them. A quick way to do this, though not as satisfying for you or your stones, is to visualize light streaming through them while affirming that they are dedicated to your healing and growth, to do only good for you and anyone else and that they will assist you in your endeavors.

Storing and Maintaining Gemstones

Though some stones are highly durable, others are quite fragile and need to be handled with care. When you are not wearing your bracelet or using your stones, they need to be wrapped in cotton or displayed where they will not be damaged. Friedrich Mohs, a German mineralogist, defined a scale (Moh's scale) for hardness, durability, resistance to scratching and related attributes (see Appendix 2)—ideally, stones of different durability should be stored separately, since the harder they are the more they can scratch or damage those less durable. Though you may love your stones just as much if they get damaged, often their efficiency for healing (and of course their beauty) is reduced when they get chipped. Fluorite and celestite are damaged even by dust, and when not in use need to be kept under glass. Try not to use polishes on gems that are mounted in silver or gold (they shouldn't be mounted in anything else).

THREE

The Root Chakra and Its Gemstones

The root chakra, *Muldhara*, is a wheel of ruby red light about three inches in diameter at the base of the spine (or more accurately, at the perineum, that piece of tissue between anus and vagina/scrotum). When developed and healthy, it extends as a funnel of red light spinning down towards the earth at the same frequency a ruby's energy spins at. Its health powerfully affects all the other chakras. Its element is the earth. Its sense is that of smell. It governs physical energy and vitality.

Often those on a spiritual quest are so eager to achieve the benefits of the higher chakras that they neglect this wonderful energy center and deprive themselves of its great gifts. If we wish to be open to grow, to feel fully alive and happy, to have good relationships, and ultimately to fulfill our potential, the root chakra is where we need to start.

Though the root chakra deals mainly with the physical aspects of our lives, neglecting it obstructs our spiritual ascent through the rest of the chakras and beyond. Contentment eludes us, we find it hard to be joyful or in a state of positive well-being, we find it hard to withstand the demands of life. We neglect this chakra at our peril.

Development

The root chakra begins developing immediately after birth, its major development occurring during the first few months of life. Though like all the other chakras it continues to mature through the rest of our lives, its thrust of growth is up to the age of three to five years old.

Root Chakra Functions

The root chakra is our foundation, supporting our energy structure and providing a secure base for our physical, emotional and spiritual health.

Survival, security and self-preservation—The root chakra keeps us alive no matter what. It is associated with the adrenal glands and the fight-or-flight response that comes into play instinctively to protect us if we're under threat.

Taking care of our basic needs—This chakra governs our eating patterns and our will to nurture and nourish ourselves adequately; our sleeping patterns and ability and willingness to take enough rest; and our motivation to provide for ourselves and to manifest what we need to live well. It also urges us to take care of ourselves wisely, dealing with our own needs before trying to help others.

Grounding—As its name suggests, the root chakra roots us to the planet, giving us a sense of attachment and belonging—provided we look after it, nurture ourselves and have direct contact with the earth. Its strong, robust earthy energy keeps us grounded and aware of our humanity even as we are spiritual beings doing extraordinary things. With good grounding we can stand against any storm.

Inner security and a sense of belonging—With the root chakra we feel we have a place in the world—we belong, we are secure and loved, we know that the earth is our home.

Sex and reproduction—The basic urge to have sex (as distinct from sexuality in general) is governed by the root chakra, ensuring the preservation of the species as well as the possibility of experiencing true orgasm.

Judgment—The root chakra helps us avoid danger in all areas of our lives while still letting us be adventurous and able to take risks.

Self-confidence and self-esteem—The root chakra supports our self-confidence and self-esteem by reminding us of who we really are—unique, magnificent, innately beautiful spiritual beings clothed for a while in a human body; wonders of creation, each with an essential contribution for the universe.

Identity—Being secure in our *own* identity allows us to celebrate the success and empowerment of others also.

Physical—This chakra governs the health and agility of the hips, legs and feet.

Healing at this chakra improves our vitality and level of energy, reduces anxiety and improves sleep. It helps us sustain the progress we make in other areas as it has the potential to shift other blocks in the system and make work at the higher centers much easier.

Being rooted to the earth, we can simultaneously draw up its nurturing energy and discharge anything negative that could otherwise cause stress and psychic overload, knowing that it will be safely handled.

Blocks or Underdevelopment

When the root chakra is weak, underdeveloped or closed, we feel lost and ungrounded; we drift without purpose, feeling of little value in the world. Very early trauma may cause dysfunction, reflected in adulthood by some of the following conditions:

Depression—Poor self-confidence, self-esteem, self-image and self-worth, together with little sense of grounding and belonging, render us vulnerable to recurrent low moods. We feel cut off from the rest of the world, lonely, isolated and misunderstood, though in reality, because of our own self-loathing, we are the ones who keep others at bay.

Ambivalence about survival—Sometimes depression is so severe that ambivalence about staying alive becomes routine and suicide seems an option. Some people may tend to opt out of life in other ways, dissociating from what's painful by drifting away emotionally and psychologically, sometimes appearing to leave their body completely.

Existential crises—Often early in adult life a person will go through periods of questioning the value of life itself and the point of being alive. Sometimes this is a precursor for a later full-blown depressive illness.

Addictions—Because of the recurrent desire to leave our painful reality, using some substance or activity that helps us absent ourselves, even if only temporarily, seems attractive, and drug or alcohol abuse or other addictive behaviors can become a problem.

Eating disorders—Eating patterns are often disturbed, characterized by under- or overeating and a disturbance of body image—how we see ourselves physically. The whole picture is compounded by low self-worth leading to self-neglect and self-harm. There is an addictive element to these disorders too.

Cynicism and negativity—The world and all in it tend to be seen in a negative fashion, devaluing both people and life, and missing the wonder of the universe.

Poor judgment—This leads us to take unnecessary risks and put ourselves in danger; sometimes this includes an element of flirting with disaster (what might be termed a "death wish") even though we are able to judge it as unwise.

Black and white thinking—Sometimes we are unable to see people as they really are—a mixture of good and not-so-good characteristics that renders them lovably human. Instead we may idealize, seeing people as completely good, or demonize, seeing people as all bad.

Physical symptoms—Stiffness, lack of graceful movement and problems in the feet, legs, thighs and hips may arise.

The Gemstones

Garnet

This deep red, often fiery metamorphic stone, noted for its toughness, is often found in potholes in river beds in many places in the world, including South Africa, Switzerland, Sri Lanka and Greece. Though it is most commonly associated with the deep red of the root chakra, in fact its color can vary through the spectrum from colorless to purple, except for any shade of blue.

Garnet has been used to protect people from harm, worn as a talisman by children and warriors. In some parts of the world soldiers still carry garnet when going into battle. When used in healing it will stimulate the heart, reducing palpitations and improving circulation. It also tends to raise the spirits and relieve sadness and mild depression, while also acting as a detoxifying agent.

When we feel that our world is shattered and we can take no more, garnet can come to the rescue—it's a great stone to have around in a crisis. It can help us galvanize our inner resources and go that extra mile—not only for ourselves but for those we love and for the community we live in. By doing so, our strength of character, self-esteem and self-confidence rise as we find ourselves capable of feats we hardly imagined. And as we move beyond our own self-limited view of who we are, we become more aware of our unique style and beauty. Old patterns of behavior are replaced by new ones; we become more dynamic, filled with ideas and the courage and fortitude to manifest them. In mind, body and spirit, garnet helps dissolve blocks, allowing us the freedom to soar and become who we really are.

Jasper

Jasper is a sedimentary rock of the quartz group and can be yellow, brown, fawn and green as well as brick red. Red jasper, sometimes also called silex, is ideal for use with the root chakra. For centuries warriors carried it in amulets to protect them in battle and to give them courage to fight a good fight. In healing it has a similar action. It helps us keep going against the odds. It helps us have the strength, grit and determination to stand up for what we believe and say what we know is true no matter what the opposition. It is useful therefore in situations where we may feel overpowered and unable to stand our ground. On a physical level it stimulates flow of both energy and circulation. A strong and robust stone, it matches the energy of the earthy root chakra.

Hematite

Hematite is dark red when ground to a powder or when the light shines through it, though in its usual form it appears black and shiny with a metallic sheen. It forms either as an igneous or a metamorphic rock. In ancient times it was called bloodstone because of its use in helping stop blood flow from wounds and in promoting the formation of blood after bleeding. Like the root chakra itself, hematite helps us survive and improves our vitality. It helps us take care of our basic needs, provide for ourselves and, like the fight-or-flight mechanism governed by the root chakra, to do whatever is necessary in a dangerous situation to protect ourselves. In physical terms, as the ancients believed, it does help stimulate the formation of blood cells and also helps with the absorption of iron. It is useful in aiding detoxification and can transform negativity. It is an excellent stone to protect against psychic attack.

Exercise

Take your stones or bracelet with you outside to where you can be with nature. Try to spend some time with your back resting against a large tree, cupping your stones in your hand, holding them against the bark of the tree. Affirm that you are renewing your connection with the earth and blending your energy with the mighty energy of the earth. Feel your root chakra, which should always remain open, and also the minor chakras in the soles of your feet. Allow yourself to feel a sense of belonging to the earth. Ask for anything you want that's connected with your root chakra—more self-confidence, greater self-esteem, a sense of family with the rest of the universe, stability, security. Ask that the earth will help heal you. You might be amazed at the sense of calm, love and peace that flows into you.

QUICK TIP

It will help you stay grounded if you keep a piece of garnet, hematite or jasper in a trouser or skirt pocket and touch it now and then with a thought to be present here and now—in the moment and in your body. Wherever you are is where you're meant to be.

Meditation

Go to the sacred space you have prepared. Take with you a glass of water, your journal and pen, and your root chakra stones or chakra power beads. Unplug the phone and give yourself at least 45 minutes of uninterrupted time. Place your cleansed stone or bracelet on the cloth or cushion in front of you where you can easily reach it, and get comfortable.

Take a deep breath, allowing yourself to breathe all the way out, letting anything negative flow out the soles of your feet and your root chakra. Relax. Take another deep breath, this time breathing in white light through the top of your head and allowing it to shine down through every cell, through every atom of every cell, cleansing, healing, balancing, bringing everything into harmony. Let yourself be filled with beautiful white light—every part of you relaxing now, feeling stronger and more connected as you allow the cares of the day to recede, leaving you free to enjoy this meditation and this ceremony to dedicate your stones. Let this time cleanse and heal you, bringing you a greater sense of inner peace and balance.

Now, with a single breath, be aware of your open root chakra. Visualize it, deep rich red, the color of the molten core of the earth. Feel your connection with the earth, your roots going deeply down into her, holding you strong and firm, giving you security, supplying your needs, ensuring your survival. Feel the strength she supports you with. Feel the welcoming way she holds you. Know you are part of her, cherished, respected, valued, and know you need to cherish, respect and value yourself also. Feel the esteem you are held in, and esteem yourself also. Feel the confidence the earth mother has in you and feel the same for yourself. Feel yourself loved—a child of the earth as well as a child of the cosmos. Like a powerful oak tree, allow yourself to absorb the robust sustenance of the earth. Feel your commitment to be here as a powerful being, to contribute to the richness of all life, essential in the balance of the universe, unique, beautiful and strong. Feel how you are part of the earth itself.

Take a deep breath and make a commitment to your survival, to meeting your needs, to taking care of yourself, nurturing, nourishing and respecting yourself. Commit if you can to being in your conscious awareness here on the planet, to willingly live out your humanity—enjoying the experience of being human and fully functioning on the human plane. Know that you are an essential and unique part of creation. Enjoy this for as long as you wish.

Now, with a single breath, open the chakras in the palms of your hands. Open your eyes and pick up your stone or bracelet. Hold it tenderly and reverently. Gaze at it and prepare to make a relationship with it. Feel appreciative of the antiquity of the stone, its beauty, the consciousness of the earth trapped in it. Allow any impressions of its history to enter your consciousness and give thanks for the strength and wisdom it is bringing into your life. Close your eyes again and cup your hands around your stones. Gently bring them into the beam of ruby light from your root chakra. Feel the gentle exchange of energy between your hands and the stones. Allow yourself to feel a warm glow of love gently spreading through your body.

Dedicate your stone or bracelet now to your healing and protection, to your connection with the earth, to your survival. Ask that this part of the earth stay with you and accompany you on your journey, that it use its healing powers for your higher good. Allow any impressions to simply float into your awareness as you silently hold your stone or bracelet; add anything you wish as you continue to make a relationship with it. Stay as long as you wish. When you are ready, give thanks, take a deep breath, and start to be more aware of your physical body. Move your fingers and toes. Return to a place behind your closed eyes, and when you feel fully aware, open them. Place your stones back on your altar or on your wrist.

Make sure you are well grounded. Take a drink of water and record your impressions in your journal.

FOUR

The Sacral Chakra and Its Gemstones

Bright orange in color, the sacral chakra, *Svadisthana*, is located about three inches below the navel. It spins out its light in front and behind us, bathing the whole pelvis and the sexual organs in its glow. Its element is water, and in good health it helps us go with the flow in all aspects of our lives. The sense associated with it is taste, and the energy, sexual expression.

Development

The sacral chakra begins its development characteristically between the ages of three and five, and we focus on its maturation until about age eight. If it develops without incident, we're likely to be flexible as adults, getting along well with others and able to bend rather than break.

Sacral Chakra Functions

Fluidity, flexibility and flow—In all areas of our lives—our moods, attitudes and opinions as well as our physical bodies—the healthy sacral chakra guarantees flexibility and flow.

Developing relationships—With a secure base at the root chakra and a strong relationship with ourselves, at the sacral chakra we can start to reach out into the world and relate with others.

Touch, nurturing, tenderness, desire and sensual pleasure—Touch is governed by the sacral chakra as well as the heart; here we start to enjoy the pleasure and nurturing of touching as well as being touched. We also begin to be able to feel sexual intimacy, enjoying the giving and receiving of sensuous pleasure.

Sexual intimacy—From the merely biological, functional aspect of sex, with its focus on procreation (the function of the root chakra), we learn to use intimacy as a form of communication, mutual comfort and nurturing. Here we refine sex and lust to desire and love.

Commitment—Though this is refined in later chakras, it's here that commitment begins as a part of the bonding that occurs when two people, each with a healthy sacral chakra, come together in any form of lasting relationship.

Internal masculine/feminine balance—Our sexuality makes integration of the masculine and feminine possible—not only as an external phenomenon. The mingling of our masculine and feminine principles also takes place *within* each of us as we develop spiritually, whether or not we have a partner, balancing the characteristics of these dual aspects of our nature.

Pleasure/pain principle—The sacral chakra helps us find the best path forward by easing the way with pleasure when we're on track and nudging us with emotional pain when we're not. It's amazing how often we fail to heed this very accurate early warning system!

Creativity—Our creativity is stimulated here, though ideas will be further enhanced at the throat chakra and manifested at the brow.

Taste—Now we begin to move out to taste life and all it has to offer.

Physical—All of our fluid systems, including the urinary system, the lymphatic and to some extent the circulatory, are governed by the sacral chakra. This chakra also governs the health of the female sexual organs as well as menstruation.

Inner Masculine and Feminine Principles

The masculine element—the part of us that deals with action, logic, organization, ambition, drive and a host of other things—is governed by the left brain, whereas the feminine functions, including verbal skills, creativity, music, art and other less structured gifts, are the domain of the right brain. Development of the sacral chakra moves us toward a state of internal balance between our masculine (action) and feminine (nurturing) principles so we feel complete. It's the fluidity of the healthy sacral chakra that facilitates constant change and movement between the masculine and feminine principles, flexibility being the hallmark of the healthy adult. In relationships this balance becomes even more critical.

Usually we choose a partner who balances our own sexuality. A man with a very strong masculine principle may look for a woman who's very feminine, whom he can take care of (rather than care for), control and dominate, and who doesn't challenge him. The woman in this relationship will be well partnered by such a man, since she has little sense of her own masculine principle and will be looking for a father-type figure to take care of her. Conversely, a man with a poorly developed masculine principle may look for a strong, dominant female who'll take charge and relieve him of much that is expected of him as a man, so that he feels less challenged within himself. The woman in this partnership is looking for someone who will allow her masculine element plenty of room.

Though these relationships may appear to give each partner balance overall, imagine what happens when either of them starts to grow spiritually and "get well." The more the internal balance of one improves, the more unstable the relationship may become. The partner is threatened and challenged and often makes counter moves to keep their loved one "sick" and thus preserve the status quo. Hopefully, as one partner begins to get well, the other is prompted to do so too. Do you recognize any of this in your relationship? If so you might like to read my book *Unlocking the Heart Chakra: Healing Relationships with Love.*

Blocks or Underdevelopment

Trauma at the time of the sacral chakra's development, or a later injury that involves this chakra, are likely to cause some of the following difficulties in adulthood:

Rigidity and inflexibility—This manifests in all areas of our lives—physical, emotional and spiritual, and in relationship with others. Though opinions are formed and governed by the solar plexus chakra, sacral chakra blocks often render us stuck in patterns of thinking, behavior and opinion. Work on both the sacral and solar plexus chakras should help the problem.

Failure to nurture—This manifests as neglect and inability to nurture both ourselves and others. Often completely unconscious, this tends to result from one or both parents being unable to nurture, which can lead to poor development of children and a trans-generational problem of neglect and sometimes abuse.

Lack of balance—Imbalance at the sacral chakra pushes us out of balance in almost every area of our lives. We often try to compensate in areas where we feel we can cope—for example, at work—but in some ways this simply makes the imbalance more obvious. Lack of inner balance between the masculine and feminine principles because of imbalances at the sacral chakra can seriously challenge relationships.

Lack of desire—Trauma between the ages of five and eight can result in an inability to feel desire and pleasure (not only sexually) in adulthood. Trauma at a later age can result in a loss of sexual desire as well as loss of interest in sexual intimacy. However, depending upon the nature of the trauma, there is sometimes, conversely, increased sexual appetite even to the point of sexual addiction—but without real enjoyment, and often accompanied by disgust and frustration.

Lack of sexual satisfaction—If the sacral chakra is sluggish or blocked, there's often anorgasmia (failure to have an orgasm), distaste for sex or loss of libido in women and erectile dysfunction in men. At the very least, sensual pleasure is harder to achieve.

Blocked creativity—Though creativity is governed to a great extent by the throat chakra (with which the sacral chakra has a special relationship), it is here that creativity is first awakened. Blocks at the sacral chakra cause a dearth of ideas that could otherwise manifest later through the throat and brow chakras.

Inability to taste—The sense associated with the sacral chakra is that of taste; often we're not only unable to taste our food, but also the other pleasures life has to offer.

Failure to heed the pain—A blocked sacral chakra tends to prevent us from hearing signals that our lives are off track, that we need to make changes and incorporate new things, human and material, into our lives.

Seeking attention—We all need attention—it's part of our need to be nurtured—but the way we ask for it is sometimes unhealthy, provoking the unkind term "attention-seeking behavior." Do you whine? Are you passively aggressive to get what you want? Do you act out your desire for attention? If so, it's at this chakra that you need to do some work.

UNDERSTANDING YOUR NEEDS AND ALLOWING YOURSELF TO HAVE THEM MET

Though we instinctively know what our needs are, blocks at the sacral chakra make it difficult to discern exactly what we do need. For instance, I may think I want food, but if I stop to examine this, I'm not hungry at all. Obviously, I have the need for something. Perhaps I'm really bored, or angry, or in pain. There are more appropriate actions for me to take than eating. Perhaps I need to meditate or go for a walk, or talk through my anger or ask someone to hug me. But because of past conditioning—for instance, when I was upset and tearful as a child, I may have been given candy or some ice cream to pacify me—I now miss some essential cognitive steps and simply go directly to the food rather than look at the cause of my discomfort. The important thing to recognize is that if you feel you need something, you do—though it may not be that chocolate bar! Unblocking your sacral chakra and taking a little time to get to know yourself will help immensely.

Physical symptoms—Stasis in the urinary tract can clog up your water-works and result in fluid retention, recurrent cystitis, infections, kidney stones, nephritis and other such problems. Blocked lymph vessels can cause swelling and tender spots on ankles and legs; circulation is not at its best and menstrual problems abound, including premenstrual syndrome. Irregular periods with or without heavy bleeding and clotting are fairly common. Since much of the emphasis of this chakra is on movement and flexibility, blocks will often result in stiffness and lack of graceful movement, particularly in the lower back, hips and legs.

The Gemstones

Carnelian

Carnelian is an igneous rock that, in its orange-brown form, is also known as sard. This protective stone comes from South America and Australia, though the best quality stones come from India. Carnelian is said to have a marked effect on emotion and mood, dispelling fear, giving us courage and diminishing irritability. It reduces apathy and makes it easier to keep calm and cheerful even when things are difficult, lifting our spirits and helping us cheer up those around us. It helps us focus and assess situations accurately, motivating us to resolve problems practically as we keep our balance, remain objective and strive to see more of the picture. It is said to aid astral travel when placed in front of a light and gazed at in meditation. Physically carnelian is a good stimulant for the circulation, encouraging good oxygenation of the tissues and therefore better nutrition. It is also said to be useful for relieving rheumatism and stiffness in the lower limbs.

Golden Topaz

Considered by the ancients the stone of Jupiter, with powers to take command of our lives and divine the truth, this beautiful magmatic stone is mined in Brazil and throughout Europe and parts of Africa and North America. Perhaps the finest quality comes from the Red Sea Island of Zebirget, east of Aswan in Egypt. Chromium gives this topaz

---

SEXUAL ABUSE

If you have difficulties with sexual intimacy because of sexual abuse in the past, there is one stone that might help you. Carry a piece of malachite with you all the time, or wear your bracelet. Malachite is also a wonderful stone for necklaces and as a pendant. You'll find more about it in the chapter on the heart chakra.

---

its stunning yellow color; however, blue topaz, containing iron, and brown or pink, containing manganese, can also be found. This stone helps us balance our emotions and control our temper, strengthens understanding and helps us move on spiritually when we appear to have been stuck. It has a marked effect on creativity, (particularly good for artists and musicians), opens inner doors for us and helps us grow and understand new concepts, leading us to emotional and spiritual fulfillment. As it strengthens our nervous system it helps us reduce fear, anger and anxiety, also supporting us in times of grief and sorrow. For those who are troubled with nightmares and ruminations that prevent sleep, topaz can be helpful. Physically it is said to be useful for stimulating metabolism and improving digestion. It has been reported to increase longevity.

Golden Tiger's Eye

This beautiful, well-named stone is a composite of limonite fibers and quartz. It has within it shiny fibers that give it its characteristic sheen. Tiger's eye has the capacity to balance the feminine and masculine energies—yin and yang—within us. It gently supports us in times of stress and trouble, helping us respond to difficulties without getting too embroiled in them. It helps us sit back, take an objective view and make good decisions, quietly remaining in our power and not being influenced negatively by others' moods. In physical terms it helps us keep calm too, slowing our metabolism slightly, alleviating pain and agitation. Because of its positive effect on the whole digestive system, tiger's eye is also good for the solar plexus chakra.

Exercise

Nurturing ourselves is essential groundwork for a healthy and fulfilling life. Work at the sacral chakra, especially using your stones, can help you put yourself at the top of your list, which in turn will help you learn how to best nurture others. Take a few minutes each day sitting with your stones and affirm that from this day forward you will be responsible for your own health and well-being; that you are aware of your own innate ability to heal yourself and that you have all the information and resources you need to be well and happy. Commit to a regular time to take care of yourself and give yourself treats. You intuitively know what you need and where changes need to be made. If you are taking some medication, don't stop it, though you may find that after some time your need for it diminishes, at which point you can discuss it with your doctor.

QUICK TIP

If your sacral chakra is not well, everything from mood to muscles feels tight and rigid and relaxation is almost impossible. You may feel tense, irritable and defensive, as you cannot truly relax. How exhausting! Why not have a bath or stand in a warm shower, holding your stone or chakra power beads and, using that special connection with the throat chakra, say or chant an affirmation or a mantra as you relax. Just let yourself flow, physically, emotionally and spiritually. An affirmation you could use is "I flow with the natural harmony of the universe and allow myself to accept all the good things it has to offer." Whatever happens will be just what you need.

Meditation

Go to your safe place and set your cleansed stones on your cloth, cushion or altar. Make sure you have a glass of water, your journal or notebook and a flower or a plant. Light your candle but make sure not to leave it unattended. Unplug your phone and give yourself 45 minutes of uninterrupted time.

Now, get comfortable and take a deep breath; allow yourself to breathe all the way out, letting anything negative flow out the soles of your feet and your root chakra. Relax. Take another deep breath, this time breathing in white light through the top of your head and allowing it to shine down through every cell, through every atom of every cell, cleansing, healing, balancing, bringing everything into harmony. Let yourself be filled with beautiful white light, every part of you relaxing now, feeling stronger and more connected as you allow the cares of the day to recede, leaving you free to enjoy this meditative ceremony to dedicate your stones. Let this time cleanse and heal you, bringing you to a greater sense of peace and inner balance.

Shift your focus to your sacral chakra; with a single breath allow it to open. See it—bright beautiful orange translucent light. Swirling energy. Visualize it extending before you, spinning and spinning, brilliant and shining. Feel the energy of this wonderful chakra. Be aware of the balance it brings. Allow your inner masculine principle to come into your awareness now—strong and powerful; magnificent and protective; strident and ardent; active and dynamic; let its might move you. Enjoy. Now become aware of your feminine principle—soft and gentle; flowing with beauty; loving and holding; nurturing and capable; wise and wonderful. Let her strength and power move you. Feel the fluid movement as these two come together and mingle in an ancient sacred dance. Feel the flowing motion, gently swirling in and around you. Let it awaken your sexuality and enliven and empower your whole being. Enjoy. Take as long as you wish to simply be with yourself and with the integration of your energy, your power, and your sexuality.

Now with a single breath, allow the chakras in the palms of your hands to open and gently open your eyes. Pick up your gemstone or bracelet and hold it with gentleness and reverence. Gaze at it, feel its energy. Recognize it as an ancient part of the earth. Feel respect for its history and for its primordial wisdom and power. Move your fingers over its surface and feel the sensuous nature of the stone. Allow a flow of love to enter into it and note any feelings in your hands or body.

Gently cup your stone or chakra power beads in your hands and bring them slowly into the beam of light from your sacral chakra, within a few inches of your body. Allow the energy from your sacral chakra and the energy of the stone to mingle. Feel a flow of love and note anything else that happens.

Let the energy help heal and protect you. Know that this part of the earth of which you are now the custodian is here to protect and nurture you as you nurture it also. Let any impressions float into your consciousness now. Feel the wonderful frequency of orange light heal you. Let it flow through your pelvis, cleansing, healing and balancing. Enjoy. And when you are ready, make a commitment to your stone or bracelet and with a flow of love, dedicate it to your healing, well-being and protection. Affirm that as you use or wear your stone or bracelet, it will bring you into harmony and balance, helping you remain flexible and fluid. When you are ready, replace it on the altar or cushion or place it on your wrist.

Give thanks.

Stay as long as you wish, but when you are ready, gently allow your sacral chakra to close. Make sure you are well grounded. Feel your physical presence, move your fingers and toes, and when you are ready open your eyes.

Stretch, take a drink of water and record your impressions in your journal.

FIVE

The Solar Plexus Chakra and Its Gemstones

Found in the upper abdomen, centrally or sometimes slightly to the left, the solar plexus chakra, *Manipuri*, is the chakra of fire. In good health it glows golden-yellow like the midday sun, radiating our power out into the world. It is also the chakra that deals with our intellect. Doing the work necessary to clear and harmonize our energy at this point releases us to move on physically, emotionally and spiritually with strength of will, power, clarity, self-assertion and purpose. This chakra governs fulfillment. The sense associated with it is sight.

Development

The solar plexus chakra develops between the ages of eight and twelve. Trauma or distress at this age can have a marked effect on us, causing us to block our feelings and find it difficult to realize our power and potential, while the prosperity that is our birthright eludes us.

Solar Plexus Chakra Functions

Power, potential, prosperity, passion, will, drive and ambition—Look at all those good things in this one chakra! We have unlimited possibilities—to work, to create change, to become what we want to be, to realize our ambitions, to be happy, to drive our lives wherever we want to go. Wow! We can let the world know we're here and we're a powerful force to be reckoned with.

Liberation—We are free to create our own life strategy in whatever way we wish. We can choose to move forward dynamically and make our lives happen, acknowledging that we are active players in whatever happens to us, and that we might as well make our vote count.

Responsibility—Taking responsibility for who we are and how we got to where we are is very liberating. If I acknowledge that I have made my life happen and I don't like what I'm seeing, at least I know I have the power to create something good instead. I only have to make a shift and commit to act always for the higher good and for peace and harmony.

Opinions, logic and belief—The solar plexus chakra governs our intellectual dimension: here we start to develop opinion and logic, to be refined later by intuition.

Prosperity and manifestation—Though manifestation culminates at the brow chakra, its seeds are sown here. We bring together our power,

DIGESTIVE FIRE

The solar plexus governs our digestive processes, letting the physical combustion of our food release energy in a form we can readily use. It is this digestive fire that gives us hunger pangs when it's high, urging us to refuel. If we learn to tune in to it, we can eat when it's at its highest (usually at midday when solar energy is at its highest), when it will burn our food efficiently, releasing all the energy available and leaving little waste to be stored as fat. When the digestive fire is low, we can eat little if at all, since our body is telling us it doesn't need to be refueled at present. Listening to this simple signal, given to us by our solar plexus, can help us maintain weight balance.

potential, will, ambition, drive, purpose and opinion to create what we want in our lives and achieve the prosperity that is our divine right.

Accommodating differences—Since we are now aware that diversity is a gift and a challenge that enriches us, we become more adept at accommodating it. Integration and cooperation enhance our lives as we find the joy in exploring the new and different.

Group consciousness—At the lower chakras we see ourselves as separate and isolated from the rest of humanity. This is individual consciousness. Now we begin to recognize ourselves as simultaneously complete individuals and yet part of a greater group. We are able to perceive ourselves as part of a team while retaining our individual identity.

Physical—This chakra governs the digestive tract—stomach, intestines, liver, gall bladder and pancreas.

Blocks or Underdevelopment

If you suffered trauma between the ages of eight and twelve, there's a good chance you'll suffer some of the following in adulthood:

Misuse of power—We've all been guilty of this at some time (even if not in this lifetime)! Power can become a dangerous weapon that we can wield over others, riding roughshod over the sensibilities of those who are less in touch with their own power. We may respond to authority figures by feeling either small or insignificant or, conversely, rebellious, superior and aggressive. Both attitudes are inappropriate.

Lack of ambition and drive—We may appear weak-willed, lacking self-determination, self-expression and direction. Drive and motivation are also affected as we studiously avoid any situation that may prompt a crisis and risk the release of the fear and pain we're trying to hide.

Helplessness—Sometimes we use our power unwisely and don't like the consequences of the choices we've made. If we feel helpless, we need to accept that we've used our power in a way that wasn't useful to us, with a result that's different from what we *really* want. If we begin to own our mistakes we can feel powerful again and change our actions to produce a different outcome. We can just as easily bring something good into our lives.

Irresponsibility—Refusing to take responsibility for our own actions undermines us and leads us to blame others for our plight. Have another look! We are not victims of circumstance, despite how it may feel, and being irresponsible only makes things worse.

"Negative" emotions—These are the feelings we don't like to feel. They include anger, rage, bitterness, jealousy, resentment and guilt. They are very potent movers in our lives if we let ourselves experience them. Blocking these émotions can be so effective, however, that the good stuff is also cut off. Love and joy, so necessary to inspire and strengthen, are lost to us when we're in desperate need of both.

Emotional wandering—If we have a blocked solar plexus chakra we may find difficulty with commitment, forming flimsy attachments because of need rather than on the basis of love. Then, because no one gets to really know us, we're deprived of the validation we so earnestly desire.

Stagnation or overflow—Stagnation alternates with overflow—either we experience little emotion, or it floods out without control. Little motivation to do anything alternates with an occasional burst of energy that leads to overtiredness and fatigue. An unwillingness to be self-assertive and say what needs to be said gives way to occasional outbursts with many basic truths spoken in an aggressive and inappropriate fashion.

Physical symptoms—Symptoms of stress abound, including irritability, disturbed sleep, lack of enthusiasm, fatigue, exhaustion, poor stamina, weight gain or loss, depression and sometimes feelings of despair. The digestive system rebels with indigestion, ulcers, acidity, constipation, irritable bowel syndrome, diverticulosis and other chronic bowel and digestive disorders. Constipation may alternate with periods of diarrhea. (My physician background needs to emphasize here that if you have such a pattern of alternating constipation and diarrhea, please go to your family doctor and have it checked out.) Since the pancreas is governed by the solar plexus, diabetes mellitus may also occur. The gall bladder and bile ducts may be blocked with stones, and abdominal discomfort aggravates the picture. Comfort eating may cause further complications as we overload the already compromised digestive system, adding to its already considerable difficulties. Obesity further lowers self-esteem. The association between repressed anger and the development of cancer has been well-documented. Does any of this sound familiar? Finally, a blocked solar plexus chakra often leads to coldness in the pelvis and lower limbs, with poor circulation and stiffness. Old arthritic pain may improve considerably when the chakra has been cleared and freed.

The Gemstones

Amber

Amber is an organic stone—dried tree resin millions of years old. For me it is one of the most precious of all the gemstones. Not only does it have such a wonderful history, and often carries within it ancient insects and pieces of vegetation, but it encourages many of the characteristics I hold particularly dear. It prompts the development of a sunny, carefree, optimistic, self-confident and flexible nature. The wearer will often be glowing with health, calm yet quick to share good humor, strong-willed but willing to listen and with the courage to change opinion, powerful but neither overpowering nor disempowering. Why wouldn't we all want to wear amber?! Amber enhances motivation and drive, but in a gentle way, so that competition is unnecessary. In physical terms amber aids all the organs associated with the solar plexus— the digestive system, the gall bladder, the liver. Amber also has a calming effect on skin irritations and on irritability. A word of caution—all that appears to be amber may not be so! Copale, which is only about two million years old, is often sold as amber but is a considerably cheaper substitute (though still nice to have).

Orange/Yellow Calcite

This beautiful waxy sedimentary stone has a long medical history. It has been used for dressing infected wounds and ulcers and for other skin disorders. It has a positive effect on those who wear it or have it in their vicinity, helping them mature spiritually and be able to see the positive in what happens in their lives. Calcite helps us trust others and ourselves and helps us motivate ourselves to get on with the job in hand even when we may not want to. Being more industrious, we find that our lives move more quickly as more of our ideas manifest, and we then tend to stretch ourselves even further to achieve. Physically calcite is good for the immune system and useful in stimulating growth in children. It acts like a tonic for those recovering from illness. It also has a positive effect on the heart, normalizing the rhythm and strengthening the beat, rather like digoxin (but if you're prescribed this medication, please don't stop taking it without consulting your physician).

Citrine

Citrine is another quartz stone that helps us keep our sunny side out, be optimistic, open, positive and face life and its challenges head on. It helps us open our lives to enjoy people and places and life in general, making us eager to experience the world and all its wonders. As we become happier, our relationships with family, friends and in business improve as does our financial security. Since it has the added benefit of quickening our reactions, citrine helps us learn and assimilate information more easily, developing our ability to make good judgments and decisions as we move on through life. Physically this stone has benefits for all the digestive tract and can have a marked effect in early diabetes mellitus (however, if you are prescribed insulin or medication, please do not stop anything—there may come a time when you and your doctor can negotiate a reduction).

Sunstone

This pretty stone, which appears to be flecked with gold, is feldspar containing tiny slivers of hematite that shine in the light. As its name suggests, this is another stone that allows our sunny disposition to shine. It helps us live out the best in our nature so we can minimize and let go of what is neither essential nor beneficial. It allows us to be optimistic and hopeful with faith in the fact that the best will happen

QUICK TIP

You can cleanse and balance your aura and help release your own power very quickly by brushing your aura with a piece of cleansed amber or citrine. If you have a power bracelet you can use it for this. If you are doing this yourself, sit or stand. If you can get someone else to do it for you while you lie down, that would be wonderful. However, make sure that neither you nor they wear any other gemstone jewelry, as the aura is very sensitive to movements within it and you are about to make a particular intention to which your aura will now respond. Take a moment to get really grounded. Then affirm your intention to manifest your true power and purpose for the higher good of all. Holding your stone or bracelet a few inches away from your body, starting above your head, gently "brush" down through your aura toward your feet with the stone. Allow yellow light to infuse your whole being as you repeat the brushing movement all around yourself, making sure the motion is always from head to toe. Give yourself a few minutes to absorb any impressions, which you can later record in your journal. Be sure to close your solar plexus chakra when you are finished and, as always, give thanks.

and we will be exactly where we are supposed to be. It has a natural antidepressant action, raising our self-confidence, self-worth and self-esteem. Physically it has a beneficial action on our whole body since it acts on the autonomic nervous system, harmonizing our whole being.

Exercise

When the solar plexus is too open, we often find ourselves picking up other people's negative energy and emotion. In particular, we can absorb anger and disquiet. So why not take your cleansed stone or your bracelet with you and spend a few minutes standing in the sunshine (wearing sunscreen and hat of course!). Just stand for a brief while with your face up to the sun and your feet well planted in the earth. (If for any reason you can't stand, that's okay—just visualize it and energy will follow thought.) Let go of any old emotions such as anger, bitterness, hatred, jealousy and resentment that no longer serve you. Discharge them into the earth via your open root chakra and the soles of your feet. Then, with a single breath, open your solar plexus. Holding your stone or bracelet in front of you, let the sun shine through it, filling it with light. As you do so, absorb the powerful energy and allow it to cleanse and heal the whole area of your solar plexus chakra and also the physical organs it governs. Affirm that you are powerful and healthy and that you are using your power for the higher good of yourself and all. When you feel ready, with a single breath allow your solar plexus chakra to close. Give thanks. Remember to leave your root chakra open.

Meditation

Go to your sacred space, taking with you your journal and pen, your cleansed stone or bracelet, and some water. Unplug your phone and give yourself at least 45 minutes of uninterrupted time. Place your cleansed stone or bracelet on the cloth or cushion in front of you and get comfortable.

Take a deep breath and allow yourself to breathe all the way out, letting anything negative flow out of the soles of your feet and your root chakra. Relax. Take another deep breath, and this time breathe in white light through the top of your head; allow it to shine down through every cell, through every atom of every cell, cleansing, healing, balancing and bringing everything into harmony. Let yourself be filled with beautiful white light, every part of you relaxing now, feeling stronger and more connected as you allow the cares of the day to recede, leaving you free to enjoy this meditative ceremony to dedicate your stones. Let this time cleanse and heal you, bringing you to a greater sense of peace and inner balance.

Take your attention to your solar plexus. Breathe gently into it and, as you do, allow it to open. Visualize it opening to reveal bright yellow light, like the midday sun. Feel its energy spreading through you, filling you with power. See yourself as the powerful, mighty being you are, capable of fulfilling your potential, being successful and living a prosperous life. Feel a glow of expectancy and excitement as you let the feeling of living a free, happy and prosperous life enliven you, opening you to greater possibilities than you have previously imagined. Let any impression of who you are and what you came here to do in this lifetime—both for you and for the planet—flow into your mind now. Feel every cell tingle as your energy moves powerfully. You are healing and being energized while you remain grounded and aware of your humanity. You are ready to face life and any challenge with optimism and courage.

Know yourself to be a powerful, prosperous being with unlimited potential. Feel your will. Know that you are capable of pushing away any self-imposed limits and manifesting the magnificent, powerful being that you truly are. Note any feelings in your body. Enjoy….

Now gently open your eyes and, with a breath, gently open the chakras in the palms of your hands; take up your gemstone or bracelet and cup it gently in your hands, allowing a flood of love to enter into it. Hold its beauty in your consciousness; let any impressions of its history enter your awareness. Feel respect for it as an ancient part of the earth. Feel the power of the earth that has been compacted within its structure. Feel the ancient consciousness of the planet here in your hands. Feel the power that you now hold. And make a commitment to use your power only for good—never to overpower or disempower, but to move all the self-imposed boundaries you have created in your consciousness and to increase your potential and fulfill your divine right to prosperity. Commit to using your will for fulfilling your purpose of experiencing being human. Breathe this intention into the stones now as you bring them closer to you. Hold them a few inches from your body in the beam of yellow light from your solar plexus. Feel the mingling of your power with the power of the universe and know that your potential is unlimited. Feel this recognition with respect and awe. Allow any impressions to enter your consciousness now.

Stay for as long as you wish, then reaffirm your commitment to the higher good and dedicate your stone or bracelet to your healing and protection. Give thanks.

With a breath ask your solar plexus to close, holding its power within you. And either replace the stones on the altar or place them on your wrist.

Be sure you are well-grounded, and when you are fully aware, gently open your eyes. Move your fingers and toes, have a stretch, take a drink of water and record any impressions in your journal.

SIX

The Heart Chakra and Its Gemstones

The heart chakra, *Anahara*, the fourth of the major energy centers, bridges the earthly and the divine—the chakras below it dealing with our humanity and those above beckoning us to our spirituality. It spins out its green light from the middle of the chest, bathing not only us, but also all we meet, in love. The healthy heart chakra helps us reassess our relationships with everything. The energy of the healthy heart chakra is what we call love, and the color of this vibration is pink; hence we can use pink as well as green stones to balance the heart chakra. Its element is air and its sense that of touch. It governs humanitarianism.

Development

The initial development of the heart chakra is between the ages of twelve and sixteen; therefore trauma that occurs during this period will have a deleterious effect on how we relate to others and how we demonstrate love and compassion.

Heart Chakra Functions

Love—Love is the most sung about and talked about topic on the planet. And yet what masquerades as love is often dependence or obsession that falls short of allowing the other person the space, support and freedom to grow as they develop and unfold spiritually. Love here at the heart chakra is sometimes without focus. This means that though we may focus our beam of love on a particular individual, we're also capable of loving everyone, everywhere—those we know and those we do not.

Compassion—This is the energy that allows us to view others with understanding, to feel their suffering and commiserate with them in their distress. However, compassion does not encompass sympathy, though many consider the two synonymous. Sympathy prompts us to make allowances, putting us on a slippery slope to collusion, which actually stunts the person's growth by hindering their ability to learn from the consequences of their actions.

Empathy—This is the ability to put oneself into the other person's shoes and feel how it must be to be them and experience what they experience. It is more than simply seeing things from the other's point of view.

Acceptance—This means being able to accept things as they are right now—and that includes myself, other people, the way they behave and what's going on in the world. However, it doesn't mean that in accepting any of it I have to like it or be complacent. In accepting, I have a piece of solid ground from which I can now decide to make changes, while always knowing that the only thing I can change is me. But if I have the courage to do that, everything else will change too.

Respect—This means I esteem the other person, have consideration for who they are and what they do. Yet in respecting them, I can still decide I don't want them in my life. With respect, parting can be with care, honor and civility.

Detachment—On the surface it seems more sensible to be attached to what we love. But at the heart of real love is freedom, which is about letting go. It's detachment rather than attachment that holds us together, as we have confidence that others can live their lives without us getting in the way and interfering with whatever process they need for their growth and development.

Bonding—Bonds develop between the heart chakras of any two people who open to each other in love. These bonds hold us in love and help us accept the other, faults and all, through thick and thin. It is also this bonding that makes separation so difficult. The deeper the love they've felt for each other, the more exquisite the pain of the loss.

Optimism—Though optimism is also associated with the solar plexus chakra, the love we feel at the heart enables us to see everyone in a new and loving light and have renewed optimism as we see the good in all people. This is not about deluding ourselves. As we communicate with the best in people, they reflect that back to us with love, and the whole world changes one smile at a time.

Forgiveness—The healthy heart allows us to forgive with understanding, love and compassion for the other, recognizing that the process they were going through and their own experience, information and emotional state led them to behave as they did. (For a discussion on the levels of forgiveness, you might like to read my book *Unlocking the Heart Chakra*.)

Physical associations—The heart chakra governs the physical heart and circulation and the chest and respiratory system; the health of this area is its concern.

Blocks or Underdevelopment

If there were problems between the ages of twelve and sixteen, it's likely that in adulthood you'll have some of the following difficulties.

Difficulties with relationships—If the heart chakra is damaged or dysfunctional, it's difficult for us to have mutually supportive loving relationships that are sustained over time. Often recurrent patterns will render relationships short-lived and painful.

Negativity and pessimism—The ability to perceive the world optimistically as a kindly place overall is often lost, and negativity and pessimism drag us down and affect those around us. As others find it difficult to relax and be spontaneous around us, we feel disappointed and rejected, depressed and vulnerable. A negative attitude is always counterproductive, as it pushes people away from us and eventually deprives us of the closeness we so desperately want.

Being critical—Those who are unhappy with themselves are often the quickest to criticize others, not realizing that in doing this they further isolate themselves by making it difficult to be comfortable around them.

Holding grudges—Since without a healthy heart, forgiveness can never be complete, arguments and disagreements are never really over, and grudges can still be held even years after the event, stopping us from letting go of the past and moving on. This usually causes us more pain than it causes the other person, and serves nothing.

Being difficult to please—This makes us difficult to be with. We're prickly and defensive and those around us feel that no matter what they do, it's never quite right, never quite enough. Often an insult or slight is perceived in almost every transaction, and though we may put this down to being sensitive, that's not really so. It's actually quite aggressive to those we relate with.

Passive aggression—On a scale of one to ten this gets ten out of ten for damaging the other person while of course depriving us of the joy of intimacy, since it puts others constantly on their guard. Passive aggression is also cowardly, since we don't have the courage to say openly what we mean, but instead make small unkind, snide comments, the real meaning of which we can then deny, accusing the other of mis-understanding and turning the tables if we're confronted about what we're really doing. In the end people around us wonder if they are going crazy as they begin to doubt their own intuition. Eventually they move away from what has become a very painful and damaging situation.

Sarcasm and ridicule—These are up there with passive aggression on the scale of damage and unkindness. Anyone who professes to love you but uses sarcasm and ridicule as a way to control needs to have their motives questioned. And if you find yourself using these, please have a look at healing your heart chakra. If there's an underlying power game, check on your solar plexus too.

Dislike, hatred, retaliation and revenge—If your heart chakra cannot perceive the good in all, it's easy to find yourself disliking other people. And if you can't really forgive, hatred also becomes an option. Both of

LOVING UNCONDITIONALLY— LOVING ENOUGH TO LEAVE...

Just as your heart chakra is the center of your chakra system, you are the center of your universe and you have a right to peace and harmony within yourself and in your relationships. Unconditionally loving someone, wanting their higher good and supporting them and their right to develop as they wish doesn't mean we have to either like their behavior or want it in our lives. There may come a time when loving unconditionally means sending them on their way. Not having the courage to do so simply prolongs the agony and enables us both to continue being hurt.

Are you in a situation where you need to make a decision to love but let go?

Are there so many areas of conflict that the situation has become untenable?

Have you done all you can to make things better and it still doesn't work?

First you need to accept things as they are and then decide what's the most loving way forward for you, remembering that your first priority is to love and protect yourself—in the end that's the most loving thing for the other person too, even if they can't see it right now.

What action would give the most loving outcome all around?

If you have to leave, how can you do it most effectively while holding on to your priority of taking care of yourself?

In almost every case we can reframe things so that there's a loving solution for all concerned, even if other people don't like our decision right now. (You might like to have a look at my book *Unlocking the Heart Chakra* and see if you can love yourself enough to do what's right for you.)

these lead us to retaliating in circumstances where we feel hurt and/ or think it's acceptable to exact revenge. It never is.

Physical symptoms—Heart and circulatory problems, high blood pressure, angina, arrhythmias and such are all possibilities when the heart chakra is blocked or traumatized. Also respiratory problems such as bronchitis, asthma and emphysema may improve when we've done the work on forgiveness, love and compassion or removed ourselves from an ongoing damaging situation.

The Gemstones

Rose Quartz

This variety of magmatic quartz develops in pale to rose pink chunks; it is classically the healing stone for the heart and in matters of love. It helps us achieve that wonderful balance of the heart where we love strongly yet gently, wisely, with compassion and empathy yet without the sympathy and sloppiness that incapacitates us and renders our love of little use to anyone. It also lets us see the romance in situations and be moved by them. This lovely stone helps us also love ourselves and open our hearts when we wish but protect ourselves from the yearning to help others that often leads us to burnout. Like aventurine, rose quartz can be used to balance and harmonize all the chakras equally. In physical terms it helps stimulate the heart and circulation while also awakening and enlivening the sexual organs by opening to potential sexually intimate partners.

Aventurine

Another member of the quartz family, this rock is colored with chromium, which gives it its delightful green. Found as either an igneous or sedimentary rock, it can be used with any chakra, though classically it is a stone for the heart. Not surprisingly, we find that it has wide-ranging healing properties. It helps us be less irritable, more accepting and tolerant so we can relax and sleep better. It helps us clarify our dreams and desires so we can manifest them. It helps us see our reality—to look objectively at what makes us happy and how we could have more of that in our lives, and what makes us sad and how we can adjust things and move into the sunshine. On the physical front it protects the heart and circulation, helping keep arteries clear of fatty plaques. The calming effect it has emotionally is also reflected in its action on skin irritations and allergies.

BURNOUT

A common "block" at the heart chakra finds it stuck wide open as we pour out more and more love around us in an attempt to heal the world. Often those in healing professions have this problem, as do many women who are so caring that they are desperate to help. The result is that they are constantly losing energy, have difficulty with boundaries and get into codependent relationships. Everyone else's pain eventually becomes too much of a burden to carry and their worst nightmare is realized as they become burnt out, ineffectual and exhausted.

Learning to close your heart chakra is as simple as learning to lift your arm. Your aura and your chakras are as much part of your body as your arm is. When you tell your arm to lift, it does so. When you tell your heart chakra to close, it will—though of course that may feel strange to you for a while, until you learn that detachment, not attachment, is what truly holds us together, and that the more you detach and allow everyone else the freedom to grow, develop and if necessary experience their own pain, the more loving you really are. Heal your own heart first—some rose quartz or malachite will help. If you're still having difficulty letting go and letting people learn to live their own lives, perhaps you could gently look at the fact that it's rather arrogant to think you're indispensable and they don't know how to cope with their own stuff if you're not around. Maybe if you step aside a little they'll have space to learn!

Malachite

Long known as the Stone of Paradise, this beautiful banded or marbled green stone is found wherever there are copper deposits. Being so beautiful, it's not surprising that one of its qualities is to help us appreciate the aesthetics of the world we live in. It also supports and intensifies the heart qualities of compassion and empathy. But its powers are more wide-ranging: It helps stimulate our wish to learn, while taking away the inhibitions that might prevent us from reaching out to become all we can be, and has a marked effect on memory, learning and the ability to grasp new concepts with ease. It helps us be discerning. Malachite earned the name "the midwife's stone" because of its action on the uterus, where it helps relieve menstrual cramps, facilitate labor and alleviate fear of sexual intimacy when there has been abuse. This stone also has a detoxifying action on the liver, and like all copper compounds, it helps ease the pain of arthritis and rheumatism. All in all, it is a wonderful stone. However, a little note of caution! The dust from malachite can be quite an irritant, causing skin and lung problems, so try to protect it from breakage and wash your hands well after handling it when you first receive it.

Other Stones

Jade, which regulates the heartbeat, improves vitality and is said to increase longevity; watermelon tourmaline helps us be less intense and soothes heartache; and emerald, which is stimulating and balancing, can also be used for the heart chakra.

Exercise

If you feel fragile, vulnerable, burnt out or just that your heart is aching, take a few stones or different bracelets—try to include some clear quartz, some rose quartz and perhaps some amethyst, though you can use whatever you have—and place them in a circle on the floor or the ground demarcating an area big enough for you to sit in. Even if you only have three stones, make a triangle. That's fine. This will set up a charged field for you to sit in. If you could intersperse some candles between the stones (tea lights or votives would do fine) that would be great, but be careful with them when they're lit. Unplug the phone and give yourself as much time as you can. Now sit in your circle and allow yourself to be just as you are. At first you may feel quite vulnerable. You might find yourself wanting to cry. If so, let it happen, knowing that the tears are bathing your soul. You are not going to fall apart forever. Allow yourself to feel protected in this circle; let the energy of the stones pour into you and heal you. Let the light from the candles cleanse and heal your aura; feel your energy start to normalize. You can do some affirmations if you wish, or just ask that you will have answers to your dilemmas or know how you can better take care of yourself. Most of all, let yourself feel the precious person you are. You deserve to have happiness and wholeness in your life. Let the earth support you and know that you are held by the heavens also. Breathe and heal. When you're ready to leave, make sure you give thanks; close down your chakras apart from your root and put out the candles. Have some water and perhaps sleep a little afterwards.

QUICK TIP

To help bring harmony and balance to those you love and to those you have loving relationships with, place some rose quartz near their photographs in your home or office, or hang a rose quartz power bracelet on the corner of the frame. Spend a moment bringing them to mind and rededicate the gemstones to making the relationship even more loving and ensuring the protection of your loved ones.

Meditation

Prepare yourself and go to your special place, taking your journal and pen, some water and your cleansed stone or bracelet with you. Unplug your phone to give yourself 45 minutes of uninterrupted time. Place your cleansed stones on a small cloth or cushion or your altar, and get into a comfortable position from which you can easily reach your stones.

Take a deep breath and then breathe all the way out; allow anything nega-tive to simply flow out of your root chakra and the soles of your feet. Relax.

Now take another deep breath, this time breathing in white light through the top of your head and letting it shine down through every cell and every atom of every cell, cleansing, healing and balancing as it goes, bringing everything into harmony. Relax. Feel yourself calming and quieting as you come into balance. Feel yourself supported by the earth, your root chakra open to hold you grounded. Feel your energy circulating, your aura shimmering and your body, mind and soul harmonizing as you let go of the concerns of the day and give this time completely to yourself. Breathe and relax.

Now take your focus down to your heart chakra in the middle of your chest; with a single breath allow it to open. Feel the chakra quicken as it spins, emerald green light shining out in front of you swirling into your aura. And notice that as your heart chakra opens it reveals within it the pink light of love. Allow this light to spill out into your aura now; diffusing through it until eventually you become surrounded by the energy of love and compassion. Feel the warmth of the love as it surrounds you, nurturing you, holding you gently. Feel yourself respond to its coaxing as you surrender to the healing power. Feel your connection to the rest of the universe, as you become part of the beam of love emanating from your heart chakra. Within this love there is the power to forgive everything—those who may have hurt you, and yourself for having hurt others. We are all part of each other's learning and growth, and those transactions were mutually beneficial even though they may have caused pain. Let them go. And if you are ready now you could flow forgiveness to wherever it needs to go and forgive yourself also for anything you are still holding on to. Breathe and let anything you no longer want to carry be discharged through your root chakra into the earth.

And perhaps if you are ready—but only if you are ready, you could raise your level of consciousness to realize that anyone who harmed you did so in the light of their own process, what they understood at the time, what they felt at the time, the information they had at the time, and that in the circumstances they could not have avoided doing so. If you are able, let forgiveness with love and compassion flow to them and to yourself. Let anything you no longer need be discharged through your root chakra into the earth. Breathe and let go.

Then if you are able—but only if you are able—you could raise your consciousness to yet another level, where you understand that you had ancient agreements with those you hurt or who may have hurt you, to help each other learn lessons, experience the tasks we chose to complete in this lifetime; that those who perpetrated some harm upon you helped change the course of your life and bring you to the greater understanding where you find yourself today. And so now, if you're ready, you can flow forgiveness to them with love, compassion and gratitude. Let go of anything you no longer want to carry and let any energy be discharged through your root chakra into the earth. You may be able to reach the point where you see that forgiveness is redundant, since we are all simply teaching and learning, giving and receiving. If you are unable to get to that point, please don't worry. We're all human beings and we have to deal with our human emotions before we can rise to the spiritual. The rest of the work need not be obstructed. Perhaps you would like to return to this meditation again when you feel more ready. Eventually it will be possible.

Now with the stones in front of you, open your eyes, and with a single breath open the chakras in the palms of your hands and pick up your stones. Hold them tenderly, reverently. Gaze at them and prepare to make a relationship with them. Then close your eyes and cup one hand over the other, enclosing the stones. Feel the gentle exchange of energy between your hands and the crystals. Let yourself feel the warm glow of love gently spreading through your body. Now draw your hands closer, holding your stones a few inches from your body within the beam of light from your heart. Note any sensations in your body or any thoughts that come into your mind. Breathe easily, simply making a note of what is happening. Now allow love from your heart to flow into the stones as you hold them before you.

Allow any impressions of their history to flow into your awareness. Feel how they are an ancient part of the earth, given into your custody gladly for your healing, for your well-being to be loved and cherished by you in return. Feel their benevolence; feel their power. Know that they will help protect and guard you, healing your heart of pain, soothing your emotions, calming your fears. Send a wave of gratitude to them now in anticipation of their service to you. Accept them now as your own—your connection with the earth, your piece of the concentrated energy of the mother. Hold them, breathe into them; commit to respecting and honoring them and dedicate them to your healing and protection.

Allow any further impressions to enter into your consciousness as you gently breathe, feeling the light, feeling the love, holding the connection. Feel compassion for yourself, compassion for the earth, compassion for the whole world. Let the love flow to you, through you and from you. Feel the stones becoming part of your energy. Breathe.

Stay as long as you wish, and when you're ready give thanks and place your stone or bracelet back on your cushion or altar or place it around your wrist.

Make sure you are well grounded. Allow your heart chakra to close to the point where it feels most comfortable and give thanks. Start to feel more aware of your physical body. Move your fingers and your toes. Start to return to a place behind your closed eyes, and when you are fully aware, open them.

Stretch and take a drink of water. When you're ready record any impressions in your journal.

SEVEN

The Throat Chakra and Its Gemstones

The throat chakra, *Visuddha*, rotates at the speed of clear, bright blue light. Though it shines out horizontally at the front of the throat, unlike the other chakras the angle is slightly raised at the back of the body. This chakra not only enables us to use that great gift, our voice, to improve the quality and purity of our communication, but also brings together the gifts of all the other chakras and helps us give them to the world. It governs speech, self-expression and the sense of hearing; its element is ether.

Development

This chakra begins its development at about 16 and continues through age 21 or so, though as with all the chakras, its maturation continues throughout life.

Throat Chakra Functions

Verbal expression—This allows us to share who we are with the outside world and simultaneously take those who hear us into our world.

We verbalize our thoughts and ideas, which, without communication, remain solitary unexpressed intangibles and, apart from expanding the mind of the thinker, have little use. As we express our thoughts we invite others to do so too in conversation—the sharing of ideas—which expands both the speaker and the listener.

Hearing and listening—This completes the loop of communication. If we actively listen, we can hear all of what is being said, every nuance, every pause and bit of verbal punctuation, deepening our appreciation of the message.

Non-verbal communication—Our understanding is further embellished by signals from the movements and mannerisms of others whether or not they are speaking to us. Sometimes the non-verbal communication tells us more than the words being spoken.

Internal communication—We also communicate internally, listening to our body and the signals it constantly gives us, listening to our soul as it gently guides us, with the universe and its higher wisdom present as a constant backdrop.

Wit and improvisation—Though to some extent wit and humor are functions of personality, the well-developed throat chakra, by linking feelings, thoughts and impressions, allows them to be expressed spontaneously.

Truth—Truth is an individual concept that depends on our knowledge, experience and understanding, and as such it is constantly developing. Though the whole universal truth is available to us all, how much of it we are consciously aware of depends on our experience and development and what we've learned on our journey thus far. Truth is therefore not a static fact, but a living, developing dynamic process that needs to be updated as we learn more and mature. The throat chakra gives us the gift of having the courage to express truth and update it as we take more of it into our conscious awareness.

Integrity—Also a personal concept, integrity depends on our current grasp of the truth, our emotional and mental state and our individual circumstances. There are things that my integrity simply will not let me do, such as dropping litter, while I might allow myself to do something else that you would consider unacceptable. Behaving in a manner that is out of line with our personal integrity costs us in guilt, shame, regret and sorrow.

Morality—Morality is also highly personal, variable and constantly developing according to our experience and circumstances. Things I may have done in my teens or twenties I would not consider moral for me now.

Creativity—A special link with the sacral chakra and the creative ideas that emerged at that lower level can now be elaborated by the throat chakra. Whatever your unique gifts, it's the throat chakra that will help you have courage to share them with the world and manifest them with the help of the healthy brow chakra.

Vocation—Our vocation is a function of our truth, integrity, creativity, desire and purpose. Though our hearts tend to lead us in the direction we need to go (and we'd be wise to follow), our brow adds intuition and our throat chakra makes living our vocation possible. The universe then rewards us with free and easy forward motion when we're on the right track, and makes us pause to think and reassess by gently (or not so gently!) placing obstacles when we need to change direction.

Clairaudience—This is the gift of inner hearing, somewhat different from hearing with our physical ears. Even those who are deaf can develop clairaudience. I personally perceive it more as a knowing that appears to come from nowhere but which I "hear" in my mind.

Channeling and mediumship—Channeling has been around for centuries, though over the last 30 or 40 years its quality has changed, as many people have opened to communicate with higher wisdom and to bring down, in language we understand, teaching about almost every subject. Mediumship tends to facilitate communication with those who have lived on Earth fairly recently.

Telepathy—This is transmitting or receiving information directly from one mind to the other without the stimulus of speech or physical hearing. We're all capable of telepathy to some extent, particularly with people we love or feel in tune with. Most mothers can tune in to their children; lovers often know exactly what the other is thinking or is about to say; most of us will have been aware of the phenomenon of intending to phone someone when they phone us. Telepathy enhances these skills. It is further facilitated by the development of the brow chakra.

Physical associations—The throat chakra bathes the neck and all its organs—the throat, vocal cords, thyroid and parathyroid glands and also the mouth, the trachea and esophagus, ears, cervical spine and carotid plexus—and ensures their good health.

Affirmations

Affirmations are positive statements in the present tense about what we want to create in our lives. At first saying affirmations may feel as though you're lying to yourself, since what you're affirming may seem far from your reality. However, repeatedly telling your mind what you are actively creating now gears up your whole being to actually create it. Sometimes the effects are astounding, though of course you need to be working on a broad front, making changes you need to make, clearing your energy and so on. The statements should be specific; they can deal with any aspect of your life (but please don't try to affirm for anyone else—with respect, what others want in their lives is their business!). The following examples show just how wide a ground your affirmations might cover:

I am creating prosperity in my life by attracting an extra $1000 every month.

My health is constantly improving as my cells work in harmony and balance, using every good nutrient for their benefit.

Divine order and harmony are quickened in my life as daily I become more aware of my divinity.

It's important that affirmations feel just right, so play around with your own words until it feels like they fit. Then you can say them daily, whenever you have a moment or at the beginning or end of your meditation, or write them in an affirmation book, making sure to date them so you can look back sometimes, check off what worked and give thanks. It's important that what you affirm is for your higher good and for the higher good of everyone else.

Blocks or Underdevelopment

If there is trauma between the ages of 16 and 21, the throat chakra is likely to be impaired in its development and some of the following may result:

Poor Communication—Either a paucity of vocabulary or torrents of words with little meaning may be typical. Also, poor syntax, flat tone, lack of clarity and a contradiction between verbal and nonverbal signals may occur. The ability to listen and truly hear all that is being said may be dulled.

Telling lies—Since there is no real acknowledgment of the truth, or the courage to tell it, lying becomes an easy option. Sometimes lying becomes such a habit that it is no longer recognized as such.

Blocked creativity—Sadly, people with throat chakra problems often have few dreams that they could manifest and find themselves living in a seemingly colorless world where everyone else appears to be having a party. What's more, they usually feel that their world is the real one and that things can never change. If you feel like that, help is at hand.

Difficulties in finding the right career—Job after job may seem promising at first but never really develops into anything that feels fulfilling and worthwhile. Purpose and vocation cannot be conceptualized.

Restlessness—Finding the right place in life is never easy, leading to restless wandering from job to job, place to place and relationship to relationship, finding little satisfaction in anything.

Living an amoral life—Developing a system of ethics based on personal integrity is difficult; therefore we may live an amoral life, or else abide by a rigid moral code that's learned rather than shaped by our own principles.

Physical symptoms—Recurrent sore throats, colds, swollen glands, neck pain and dental problems may be prevalent. There may be symp-

MY PERSONAL EXPERIENCE

Some years ago, when practicing full-time as a clinical psychiatrist and doing workshops and seminars on weekends and in my vacation, my soul constantly nudged me to make changes and spend more time channeling, healing, writing and teaching. However, for a year or so I failed to act on what I knew to be right for me. Then the universe decided to prompt me a little. Over a six-week period I had a car wreck (no one was hurt), fell downstairs in the hospital and developed a gynecological problem. I then decided to take a sabbatical and began to write my first book. Those messages from the universe were wonderful—though it might have been better if I'd heeded the signs earlier.

toms of hypo- or hyperthyroidism. The former presents with lethargy, weight gain, low mood and coarsening of skin and hair; the latter with weight loss, anxiety, poor sleep and increased energy that's accompanied by jitteriness.

The Gemstones

Turquoise

This sedimentary stone, mainly aluminum phosphate colored by copper and traces of iron, originally came mainly from Iran, and derived its name from the Turks who carried it. It was also used in South America, where it was considered so sacred that originally it was only used as an offering to the gods and as a decoration of their images. For generations it has been used by some Native American people as a protective stone, protecting its wearer from injury, deepening meditation and clarifying intuition, bringing happiness, good luck and prosperity while also preserving love and friendship. It promotes inner calm and peace with heightened awareness. It helps alleviate pain and has an anti-inflammatory and anti-viral action, while increasing circulatory flow to muscular tissues, particularly if worn on the fingers as rings. It's said to be useful in the treatment of anorexia nervosa, having an overall stimulant and regenerative effect on the body. Useful also to protect us from pollutants, it is said that its color changes depending upon the health of the wearer.

Fluorite

Mainly a magmatic rock, fluorite is found in various locations around the world; its color ranges from violet to green, yellow, pink or blue, depending on the minerals at its site of development. Fluorite helps us stand up for what we know to be right and speak out with integrity against oppression and injustice. It stimulates our creative capacity and prompts us to manifest in our lives all that we're capable of. In so manifesting, we become more self-confident as we bring together our existing knowledge and update it, taking on new concepts with ease and opening to greater depths of meditation with new insights. Physically fluorite acts on several systems of the body, including the skin and mucous membranes, the respiratory tract, the joints, bones and teeth and the central nervous system. Overall its action is regenerative, healing tissue and bringing renewed mobility. Fluorite can be scratched very easily; it would be better to have it as a gemstone rather than fashioned into a bracelet.

Blue Lace Agate

This gentle, seemingly innocuous stone has great qualities that reach into almost every system. It has always been seen as a stone that brings good fortune. It also helps us remain centered and calm while contemplating our affairs and determining how to proceed in a mature, well-controlled and less emotional manner, sorting out what is important and essential and what can be discarded as we move on. It helps us be logical and analytical, able to make decisions and implement them effectively in line with our integrity. A powerful stone for cleansing and stabilizing the aura, blue lace agate promotes generalized good health. It influences various organs positively, including the skin, the eyes, the stomach and digestive tract, the bladder and the uterus. It reduces inflammation, stimulates healthy growth, and is useful after childbirth to help the tissues, especially the uterus, regain their strength and elasticity. This stone is so powerful that much of its activity can be felt by merely having it in your vicinity, though of course wearing it on your skin intensifies its benefits.

Also for the Throat Chakra

Aquamarine, which tends to reduce stress, help us think more clearly, improve creativity and protect us against pollutants, can also be used for throat chakra; the wearing of silver enhances this chakra's function.

Exercise

Whatever you do, you could make it a rule that you always give gratitude with your voice. Though inner thanksgiving is fine, and there are times when a silent prayer is proper, you can open your throat and give gratitude at any time. Opening our throat to sing ennobles us, but the best thing about doing this is it clears our throat chakra and therefore shifts blocks that otherwise impede communication, creativity and higher gifts. So if you can sing, fine. But even if you feel you can't, you can chant or learn a mantra to repeat in a rhythmical way that will open up your throat just as much, helping bring considerable changes into your life. If nothing else, say your affirmations out loud. I always say mine when stuck in a traffic jam and seemingly have nothing else to do!

QUICK TIP

Fluorite can be used as a tool to help learning. To energize your workspace, improve your productivity and increase your capacity to learn, arrange your desk according to *feng shui* principles and place your piece of fluorite on it. You will find that not only will your space feel lighter but you will feel much more creative and able to communicate succinctly and effectively.

Meditation

Go to your special place, taking your journal and pen, a glass of water and your cleansed stone or bracelet with you. Unplug your phone to give yourself 45 minutes of uninterrupted time. Place your cleansed stones on a small cloth, cushion or your altar and get into a position that is comfortable for you and from which you can easily reach your stones.

Take a deep breath; breathe all the way out, and allow anything negative to simply flow out of your root chakra and the soles of your feet. Relax. Now take another deep breath, this time breathing in white light through the top of your head; let it shine down through every cell and every atom of every cell, cleansing, healing and balancing as it goes, bringing everything into harmony. Relax. Feel yourself calming and quieting as you come into balance. Feel yourself supported by the earth, your root chakra open to hold you grounded. Feel your energy circulating, your aura shimmering and your body, mind and soul harmonizing as you let go of the concerns of the day. Give this time completely to yourself. Breathe and relax.

Now, with a single breath, allow your throat chakra to open. Visualize it— spinning and spinning, revealing blue light shining out in front of you and behind you. See the sky blue or turquoise light surrounding your throat and your neck, your shoulders and the lower part of your face. Feel the cool blue light bathing all your organs of communication. Feel clarity and lightness around your throat, your mouth, your tongue, and your ears. Know that your communication is improving so that you can speak with clarity and command, with gentleness and tenderness, with truth and integrity. Know that you can speak your message to the world. Know that if you wish you can also hear—truly hear—the messages lovingly sent by your fellow travelers and the messages from the universe. Ask now anything you want to know and know that your soul will reply, if not now, later. Listen for a moment and allow the impressions of who you really are, what you are here to learn and what you are hear to say to enter into your consciousness. Hold the clarity. Breathe it in and breathe out into it. If the lightness feels strange, simply be more aware of your grounding and breathe. Feel your power and know that in this moment you are moving closer to accomplishing your purpose. Allow positive feelings about this to come into your consciousness and simply note them without trying to hold them. Feel your whole being and enjoy.

Stay as long as you wish; when you're ready, open your eyes, and with a single breath allow the chakras in the palms of your hands to open. Take up your gemstone or chakra power beads. Look at them and appreciate their beauty. Let a flow of love from your heart wash into them. Be open to receive their love for you also. Gently cup your hands around them and bring them into the beam of blue light a few inches from your throat. Allow the power and clarity of your throat chakra to gently mingle with their power; allow any impressions to enter into your consciousness. Hold the exchange of energy as your clarity is enhanced by the power and beauty of the stones. Make a commitment to increasing your clarity even further, to improving your communication in all ways, to remembering that sometimes the best com-munication is loving silence and not torrents of words. Commit to improving communication with everyone you meet, to moving more and more into line with your purpose day by day, living in your integrity, living your purpose, living your vocation.

Allow a mingling of the energies. Let any impressions simply float into your awareness without thinking about them. Hold them lightly. Know that there is healing of the area around your neck, your throat, your thyroid, your mouth, ears, nose and throat.

Stay as long as you wish, then give thanks; when you are ready, simply allow your throat chakra to close, holding newfound clarity within. Now gently replace the gemstones or bracelet on the altar or cushion or place them on your wrist.

Make sure you are well grounded. Have a drink of water and record your impressions in your journal.

EIGHT

The Brow Chakra and Its Gemstones

Sometimes erroneously called the third eye, the brow chakra, *Aina*, is located above and between the physiological eyes. Its color is deep indigo blue like the night sky, though sometimes it has a purple tinge. It is the chakra of inner vision and intuition, where we take command of our life, our learning and our dreams. The brow chakra brings all the others together in readiness for the final ascent to the crown, where spiritually we may finally reach full bloom. Its element is telepathic energy and its sense is that of intuition. It governs psychic power.

Development

Though this chakra may begin its development at about the age of 21, some of us never develop it in this lifetime. Occasionally, however, precocious development occurs in young spiritual people who are psychic, and sometimes it begins its development spontaneously in our 40s and 50s or even later.

Brow Chakra Functions

Vision, insight and perception—Though the brow chakra covers the anatomical and physiological pathways of physical sight, it's also the place for inner vision, inner sight—in-sight. We can also have visions for the world, as we perceive everything more clearly and with greater ease, beyond the normally accepted bounds of the senses. Now in a boundless, timeless universe, we have a clear picture of who we are and what we can create.

Inspiration and devotion—The brow is also the place of devotion and being in spirit—in-spired. Here we become more aware of our connection with the Divine and of our own divinity. In our meditation or prayer we find a new reverence, almost a tearful joy, coupled with excitement. Here we begin to feel devotion. But not only that, here we may become aware of great souls and angelic presences around us, welcoming us and helping us carry divine love to whomever we meet. In devotion we may be flooded with ideas, with energy, with wisdom, with knowledge, or we may be transfixed and simply held in love and peace.

Intuition and psychism—Everyone is intuitive, though many of us ignore this wonderful sixth sense. Though we use it unconsciously all the time, we can take conscious command and use it as a powerful tool. At the solar plexus we had raw gut feelings. Here they can be refined and honed to perfection, allowing us to learn to dip into the ocean of knowledge we live in and interpret signs from the universe that often go unnoticed. (You might like to read more about this in *Unlocking the Heart Chakra*.) In many ways, being psychic is simply an elaboration of intuition. We have the solutions to all problems, even though as yet they may not have been posed. We have the answers to all questions, even though as yet they may not have been asked. With a little courage and minimal training we can start to use our psychic skills to tap into areas that until now we may have felt are only available to a select few. But we need to be ready to treat such skills with respect and reverence and to have a strict code of ethics so as not to abuse anyone's privacy.

Wisdom—At the brow chakra we're blessed with the combined wisdom of all our previous experiences. Though even greater under-standing is yet to come at the seventh chakra, here we have wisdom beyond anything that can be taught, beyond intellectual knowledge, beyond academic learning.

Clairvoyance—This spiritual gift allows us to see clearly beyond the horizons of time and space. Anyone can learn to use clairvoyance to some degree, given time and the will to work on it.

Light and color—As we have seen, light and color are tools used to heal and balance the whole energy system. In choosing gemstones to match the colors of the chakras, we have found that their healing properties, in general, support and emphasize the qualities of the relevant chakra. This comes from the similarity in their frequency.

MEMORY

Memory is governed by the brow chakra and, as you clear this area, you may experience a flood of long-forgotten memories. If these are painful, remember that you have survived the reality and will now survive the memory. There are three main types of memory:

Intellectual memory, either short term or long term, lets us remember what we did yesterday or in childhood, and how to find our way home.

Physical memory is a factor of our cells storing memories in their tissues. As my body remembers a situation, it may react to some similar event, even though intellectually I may have no recall of it. An example of this is the pelvic numbness often felt by women when they try to make love, if they have suffered sexual abuse in the past.

Feeling memories may surface when, for example, we feel anxious or afraid in a particular situation even though we have no intellectual memory of having been in a similar situation before. The intellectual memory has been repressed, but the feelings remain. Being aware of these different types and levels of memory can help us sort out what's happened to us in the past and what we need to heal.

Some memories go beyond the bounds of this lifetime and are in fact from past lives.

Magic, miracles and manifestation—At the brow we are reintroduced to our true power as spiritual beings. This is different from the power of the solar plexus. Though the affirmations of the throat chakra remain important, the brow chakra takes manifestation a stage further. As we develop or heal the brow, we begin to project powerful images into the world and make them our reality, manifesting for the higher good of all, almost with a thought.

Healing—Energy follows thought, and here, as long as we have a healthy heart chakra, with a thought and a vision for the higher good of others, we can send out powerful healing to the farthest corners of the planet.

Mind messages—Each time we think lovingly of someone, the thought energy goes off into the ether like a recorded audiotape to eventually reach them. The recipient of our message will suddenly think of us also and may return the message with a pleasant smile and love. We can learn to do this more formally if someone is willing to be a transmitter and another the receiver, though its practical application is small (except for shows and parties!). This is a further development of telepathy, which we discussed in the last chapter. Beware of sending negative thoughts!

Physical Associations—The brow chakra governs the eyes, head, neck and ears. It is connected to the pineal gland, which orchestrates the whole endocrine system and also secretes melatonin, which promotes sleep.

Blocks or Underdevelopment

The brow chakra can function quite well in some of its aspects even if underdeveloped or blocked. However, even intellectual brilliance can be improved by the addition of wisdom, self-awareness and the ability to transcend rational thought. Unfortunately, traditional education sometimes dulls intuition and creativity and teaches us to undervalue what cannot be scientifically proven. Maybe we simply do not have sufficiently sensitive instrumentation with which to measure the mystical!

Inability to follow through with creative ideas—If we have a block or lack of development at the brow chakra, we may have good ideas but appear surrounded by plans that never quite come to completion. We may make promises we cannot keep and be unaware that we fail to honor commitments and of the frustration this causes others.

Blaming others for our shortcomings—Sometimes we may project our own frustration and blame others for the mess of half-fulfilled plans we find clogging our lives.

Stunted vision—Though we might perform well in a restricted environment where we can assume a great degree of control, we're rarely able to open to a greater vision, tending to plagiarize others' ideas instead.

Ridicule—If we have a blocked brow chakra, unlimited joy eludes us and we're inclined to ridicule those who can experience such joy, dismissing it as a delusion or a flight of fancy, demanding proof and reducing everything to the material.

Putting others down—Though of course we'd be quick to deny it, sometimes having a brow chakra block makes us so insensitive that we can cruelly trample on the finer emotions of those who are open to seeing things in a different way. Sometimes we seem bent on trying to prove that our negative view of the world is correct.

Seductive with words—Powerful communicators, bright and affable, people with blocked or underdeveloped brow chakras may nevertheless offer seductive arguments.

Physical symptoms—The area most affected by a sixth chakra block is vision; eyestrain, conjunctivitis, headaches, migraines, poor sight and even blindness may occur here. Difficulties with memory may arise. Since the pineal gland secretes melatonin, which stimulates sleep, sleeping difficulties are also common. With this chakra more than any other, a problem may show little if any physical evidence, though sometimes nightmares or epilepsy provide clues.

Sometimes people with brow chakra problems can unblock quickly if their world becomes threatened either by illness of a loved one or by loss, through calling on God or higher powers for help. For a while they may become quite zealous in their newfound "religion." Usually this is short-lived, however, since they have difficulty surrendering to the work they need to do to really change their lives.

The Gemstones

Lapis Lazuli

This beautiful deep blue stone from Afghanistan, Russia, Chile and North America, mentioned as a cure for cataracts as early as 1600 B.C., is a metamorphic rock made up of several minerals including lazurite, sodalite and calcite; it often has speckles of iron pyrites. It's said to have a natural antidepressant action, to increase awareness and raise self-esteem. Lapis is also good for helping release creativity and self-expression. It has a protective action and is wonderful when working with the brow chakra, enabling us to tap our psychic abilities. Work with past lives is enhanced by lapis—I used it constantly when starting to work with my patients doing past-life regression. This stone had

IN FOR SOME TOUGH NEGOTIATIONS? SUGILITE MAY BE THE ANSWER

Sugilite (luvulite), sometimes known as the healer's healer, always has a place in my consulting room since it holds the energy perfectly and absorbs anything negative that might be released while I'm working with clients. It's also very pretty! Its beautiful purple makes it perfect for work with either the brow or the crown. However, it is quite rare, and was discovered only in the last 50 years in Japan (it is also found in South Africa). It's good to use when there is a power struggle, negativity or when someone is being domineering since it helps us maintain our point of view despite pressure to change and also to help find agreement in conflict. Carry a piece with you or have it on the boardroom table during tough negotiations!

a powerful effect in allowing me to see their past life experiences simultaneously with them. It also let them quickly clear issues that had past life origins. Though I now "see" with my clients automatically, I highly recommend lapis to you if you want to train in this work. Though some healers prefer unpolished stone, I've found that the polished stone works just as well. Lapis is also a powerful gemstone for aiding meditation. Work on the brow chakra with it may be useful for dementia and epilepsy (but don't stop your medication without negotiating with your physician) and can improve vision. This stone has an analgesic effect and can be good for headache (though if you have recurrent or persistent head pain, please see your doctor) and neuralgia. It's also said to be useful in preventing miscarriage, so if you or someone you know has such a problem, you'd have nothing to lose by trying it. Finally, lapis lazuli helps cement friendship. Like jade, it is better received as a gift rather than bought.

Amethyst

Another favorite of mine, and something I wear almost daily, amethyst is a wonderful transformational aid when used with either the brow or crown chakras. It helps us be constantly spiritually aware, and during meditation it helps us open to previously unattained levels. It helps us clear our own vision, enabling us to see more clearly for the benefit of others too; therefore, for a practitioner, amethyst is undeniably one of the great gemstones. It helps us have a sense of justice and fairness while stimulating our innate wisdom and bringing a sense of peace. It protects us from negativity by absorbing any unwanted frequencies around us, and also clears the aura of pollution (so please wash it regularly, since it works so hard for you). It has a marked calming effect (put a piece in the corner of your pillowcase—it might stimulate dreaming for a few nights and will then help promote serene sleep) and helps us feel content with our lot. Amethyst is a good gemstone to use when grieving, since it helps us come to terms with loss.

Sodalite

This is the gemstone of freedom, where we take what is rightfully ours and free ourselves from anything oppressive that would prevent us from being who we are. Increasing spiritual awareness, sodalite also helps us be detached and objective, pressing us to find truth as we follow our ideals and live the life we know to be right for us. This stone can lift our spirits and help us see things in a lighter, more positive way, getting things into perspective and being more laidback and easy-going—useful, since our intensity can wear other people out! Sodalite also has a balancing effect on our metabolism. It can also be used for the throat chakra, where it helps the voice and relieves throat complaints such as hoarseness.

QUICK TIP

When not wearing your power bracelet, hang it in the window where it will catch the light, and it will be cleansed and energized for the next time you want to wear it.

Exercise

We have access to the answers to all the questions we will ever need to ask—so if you have some problem or dilemma, you might like to try the following:

Have your notebook or journal with you and lie down where you won't be disturbed. Place a piece of lapis lazuli, amethyst or your cleansed and dedicated deep blue power bracelet on your forehead. Close your eyes and focus for a moment on your breathing. Breathe deeply and calmly and imagine light coming in at the top of your head and being released out through the soles of your feet. Know that you have all the wisdom you need for finding the solution to your problem or dilemma. Now, with your eyes closed, look out through your brow chakra and ask to "see" or know the solution that is for the higher good of all. Allow anything to come into your mind—just note it and let it go rather than grasping it and thinking about it. Your unconscious mind will remember it. Even the most odd and seemingly unrelated ideas may later turn out to be relevant. Stay only a few minutes—five at most—then give thanks; allow your brow chakra to close. Sit up, have a drink of water and record everything you can remember, no matter how strange.

Then spend a few minutes interpreting it in light of the dilemma you have. If there seems to be no association right now, don't worry—there will be later.

Meditation

Go to your sacred space, taking with you your journal and pen, your cleansed stone or bracelet and some water. Unplug the phone and give yourself at least 45 minutes of uninterrupted time. Place your cleansed stone or bracelet on the cloth or cushion in front of you and get comfortable.

Take a deep breath and allow yourself to breathe all the way out, letting anything negative flow out of the soles of your feet and your root chakra. Relax. Take another deep breath, this time breathing in white light through the top of your head and letting it shine down through every cell, and every atom of every cell, cleansing, healing, balancing and bringing everything into harmony. Allow yourself to be filled with beautiful white light—every part of you relaxing now, feeling stronger and more connected as you let the cares of the day recede, leaving you free to enjoy this meditation and this ceremony to dedicate your stones. Let this time cleanse and heal you, bringing you to a greater sense of peace and inner balance.

Now, with a breath, allow your brow to open and let the deep richness of the indigo light bathe your brow. Feel the light spread through your head, spill around you and shine out in front of you—deep blue, velvety light like a darkening sky, rich in its majesty. This light holds in it your power of vision. With your eyes still closed, look out through the beam now. Visualize your path. See your way forward. Feel the power of moving down your spiritual path, knowing who you are, why you are here and how you are to get your message out into the world. Others are here to support you, to help, cherish and nurture you. You already know some of them; some are just entering your life now. Welcome them with love and gratitude with a commitment to the higher good of all of you. Allow the highest vision of your purpose to come to you—of your place in the unfolding wonder of the universe. As the vision enters your consciousness, hold it gently without judgment, without grasping—simply be aware. Breathe into it and allow it to settle in your being. Give thanks for it.

Stay as long as you wish. When you are ready, gently open your eyes and, as you do so, allow the chakras in the palms of your hands to open. Take up your gemstone or chakra power bracelet and look at it. Gaze at its beauty. Feel its history; feel its power. Feel the consciousness of the planet that is held within it. Allow yourself to accept in gratitude and awe that you are now custodian to this part of the planet. Allow an exchange of love and respect.

Now, cupping it in your hands, bring it into the beam of light from your brow chakra and hold it a few inches from your body. Let any impressions simply flow into your awareness. Simply observe, allowing the space and freedom for anything that is for your higher good to manifest. Now give thanks and make a commitment to respect and honor your gemstones, allowing their power to enhance your vision and enabling you to really see—to open to the greater vision for yourself and the whole universe, to move in line with your true purpose. To marry your passion with desire and really make your mark in the world. To improve your intuition and help you see beyond the physical. To bring wisdom to everything you do and help you open to respect the vision of others too.

Hold your vision and allow any impressions to simply drift into your consciousness. Observe them gently.

Stay as long as you wish, and then when you're ready, gently allow your brow chakra to close; replace the stones on the altar or cushion or place them on your wrist. Give thanks. Make sure you are well grounded, have a drink of water and record whatever you wish in your journal.

NINE

The Crown Chakra and Its Gemstones

The crown chakra, *Sahasrara*, is the "thousand lotus blossom" chakra, found at the top of the head, protected with elaborate headgear by ancient kings (a practice that still lingers in the wearing of tiaras, coronets and crowns by royalty). At the crown chakra we open fully to our spirituality, to unity consciousness and to our divinity.

Development

Though the crown may begin its development after the age of 26, in many of us it hardly develops at all until perhaps the last few moments before death, when at last we realize the full extent of our consciousness and divinity. There are no blocks to the crown chakra: we are either able to open to its glories or we are not ready for its wonder. Whether or not it is developed, we can still visualize light coming in through it and make use of the healing light from the Divine. For some people, working on the crown chakra is a life's work.

Crown Chakra Functions

Universal consciousness—Here we finally become aware of the meaning of unity consciousness—sometimes known as universal, Christ or Buddha consciousness. We realize that we are all one, that we are simultaneously human and divine and that everything is in divine order. Here we are aware of the limitless, boundless nothingness that encompasses everything; here we know that there is no space between us, and yet there is only space—that we are merely bodies of light. Here we become aware of consciousness that is invisible and yet visible in everything there is.

Understanding—In reaching unity consciousness an understanding that goes beyond anything we could learn or surmise with logic arises.

Peace, ecstasy and bliss—From here we can learn to transcend beyond all we have known thus far. We can program ourselves to reach the unreachable, to touch the untouchable and to find, albeit initially only for tiny snatches of time, absolute peace, where everything is suspended and we have utter awareness. This is where we can experience ecstasy.

Transformation—When we learn to hold this state for longer and eventually live it simultaneously with our human life, something wondrous happens to us. We are transformed—permanently changed. We have glimpsed and experienced heaven and we can never be the same again.

Radiating love and peace—When we have mastered the art of working with the energy of the crown, for the most part we can be calm and serene, radiating universal love to all those around us. Though this takes time, dedication and patience, it's worth every bit of effort. But don't forget, even when we've reached that place, we remain ordinary human beings, doing ordinary things with our feet on the ground. And we're not expected to float around constantly in a state of beatific peace! We are human beings with human emotions—it's part of our business on earth to feel them.

Knowledge and truth—In the same way a seed contains the whole template of the plant and the strand of DNA holds the key to the whole person, this moment holds all the truth and all the knowledge there ever

THE CROWN CHAKRA AND ITS GEMSTONES   87

ALIGNMENT

We've been looking as the chakra system bit by bit to understand its functions, its gifts, and perhaps why it hadn't been working as well as it might. But now we can look at the whole system in one piece. Here we may now have seven unobstructed chakras that, joined centrally by the vertical current running up the spinal column, form a clear channel. Now you can see (and maybe feel) how easy it is to allow a breeze of energy to blow up and down through them all, enlivening them and symphonizing all our gifts so that we can use them and bring ourselves harmony and bliss. We can have the rise of energy from the earth and the arrival of spiritual energy from above. This alignment is possible all the time, but particularly when we meditate. As it connects us with the Divine, we become who we really are—humanity and divinity in perfect manifestation and balance. Wonderful!

was and ever shall be. All we have to do is find it. We are all at different points on the path; our primary goal is to reach a point of knowing.

Enlightenment—Here at the crown, we're suddenly able to be free of the constraints of our human brain and can immerse ourselves in truth and knowing as we transcend and are at one again with the great body of consciousness, the divine source we may call God. Here at last we can be enlightened as we surrender with simultaneous power and humility to that which is so much greater than us and yet of which we are a powerful part.

The Gemstones

Clear Quartz

This stone that was at the heart of the Atlantean civilization (see Appendix 1) is the most ubiquitous and versatile of gemstones. The universal healer, clear quartz can be can be used to heal and balance any chakra since its energy is so clean and pure. Used alongside any other crystal, it will amplify the other's energy. It can enhance any of the functions of the crown chakra and stimulate the swift ascent from the brow to the crown, quickening the manifestation of psychic and spiritual gifts. It receives, transmits and stores information. It has so many positive actions physically, emotionally and spiritually that they're difficult to list. Suffice to say that no one should be without it. It is found in the clear male form or the softer milky feminine form, which is less strident in its action. Because of its stimulant action, it's unwise to have it in your bedroom, where it may keep you awake. Since the male stones in particular are highly stimulant to cellular growth, I consider it better to use amethyst or spectrolite for crown chakra work where someone has cancer, since there's a possibility that clear quartz may stimulate the growth of malignant cells too. Clear quartz is purported to be useful in helping nerves regenerate, and therefore it may be useful with numbness or paralysis.

Labradorite (Spectrolite)

Though this gemstone is basically green, gray or black, it is iridescent with all the colors of the spectrum when it catches the light, and is such a wonderful stone for the crown chakra that it must be mentioned here. It has the same frequency as the crown chakra and helps clear and open the crown, stimulating channeling and intuition. It also helps us clear old debris that may stand in the way of our ascent. It helps us with telepathy, inspiration and intuition. An aid to meditation, labradorite protects the aura and promotes peaceful sleep. It acts on the pineal and pituitary glands, the liver and the lymphatic system. It also has wonderful protective qualities; it's another one that I love to wear regularly, especially when I'm working.

Celestite

Celestite's name means heavenly, and this soft and fragile colorless or white stone helps us make and hold a conscious connection with the Divine. As we awaken our spirituality, it helps us transcend. During meditation it helps us suffuse our energy body with light and love. In its pale blue form celestite is good for the throat chakra, where it improves communication, helps release our creativity and heightens our awareness while also having a healing effect on the thyroid. Too fragile for jewelry and easily damaged by handling and water, it needs to be carefully stored. It is wonderful for the meditation room. On occasions I have placed it under the couch on which I'm working with a client—with very good results, since it aids memory recall, healing old feelings as they emerge. Make sure you are constantly aware of your grounding, and if you use it with a client, make sure she is well-grounded before leaving your room.

Amethyst

Though we discussed amethyst in the last chapter, it is another stone that's superb for work at the crown.

Diamond and Herkimer diamond are also ideal for use with the crown chakra.

Exercise

Now you're going to have a go at channeling, so this is really more than an exercise! You'll need to have some recording device by you, whether that consists of notebook and pen, a tape recorder or a friend you can trust to simply be there and scribe for you without making any comment (and certainly without bursting into laughter!). At first it will help to hold a crystal or gemstone you have dedicated for this very purpose (simply cleanse it, and when you do the meditation to dedicate it, do so for channeling rather than for your healing and protection).

Please always begin by being grounded and by asking that you receive only the highest and the best energy, information and guidance. Allow yourself to stand aside—this may sound strange until you actually do it. My personal experience is that Brenda stands just a little in front of me and to the left while I prepare to open my crown chakra and become still with an inner silence. My breathing becomes different, usually quite shallow and sometimes hardly there at all; then I trust that whatever happens will be right and

I simply relax into the process, but with great respect, reverence and gratitude for the privilege of being able to have this contact. I then let myself literally be used as a channel for information to flow. Opening my mouth to let the information be manifest through my throat chakra or putting it down on the page doesn't disturb the flow. I can channel while writing on my computer too. When you begin, you may find that you have a stream of consciousness flow through you, then it seems to stop and you lose the connection. That's okay—it's usually that your ego starts to get in the way and question what's happening. You'll be able to tell immediately if that happens. It's almost as though you hit the earth with a bit of a thud and you're back here feeling a bit foolish because you don't really know what you were talking about. That's okay. Just center yourself again, and off you go. I often find myself listening to what's coming out of my mouth almost as an audience, knowing that it's completely separate from me. Sometimes if I'm channeling for someone else I have no idea at all what's been said—quite disconcerting for the other person!

When you feel that it's over for now, or you're tired and want to stop, all you have to do is to have that thought and move back into place, and there you are. Give thanks. Get grounded again. Feel your physical body, have a drink of water, stretch and take your time before you do anything else.

A handy tip: While you're channeling, don't worry about what you're saying, what's happening, how accurate it might be or that you might be making a fool of yourself! Just report it as it is. Sometimes I've reported things that appear to make no sense but turn out to be significant to someone else. Try not to interfere with the process or you'll lose the connection. Please respect the sanctity of the process, and until you've mastered the art, don't attempt to channel anything for anyone else. No party games please!

Meditation

Go to your safe place and prepare yourself. Place your cleansed gemstones or chakra power beads on your cloth, cushion or altar. Make sure you have a glass of water, your journal and pen. Light your candle and make sure that you do not leave it unattended. Unplug your phone and give yourself 45 minutes of uninterrupted time.

Now, get comfortable and take a deep breath; let yourself breathe all the way out, allowing anything negative to flow out of the soles of your feet and your root chakra. Relax.

Take another deep breath; this time breathe in white light through the top of your head and allow it to shine down through every cell, through every atom of every cell, cleansing, healing, balancing and bringing everything into harmony. Allow the light to fill every part of you, relaxing now, feeling stronger and more connected. Breathe a long sigh and with it let go of any cares you may have. You can pick them up again later if you really want to. Your subconscious mind will remember anything you need to know, so just abandon yourself now to the ceremony you are about to perform.

With great reverence gently allow your crown chakra to open. As you do you will feel a flood of divine love flowing down into you and filling you with warmth, clarity, wisdom, understanding and knowing beyond intelligence and thought. Feel this connection as white light pours into you, around you and from you. You may be aware of violet light around you. Simply let any positive impression float into your awareness and enter into your consciousness. Be sure you are well grounded. Feel the energy flowing through you, lifting your consciousness, filling you with a love that carries a quality you've never previously known. Feel yourself flooding with energy as white light bathes every cell—a river of energy connects you with the Divine. The connection holds you now in your own divinity—wonder at the magnificence of your divinity and humanity combined. Feel yourself as the amazing spiritual being that you are. Know yourself in your magnificence as the benevolent divine love bathes you, heals you and brings you into perfect balance.

Stay as long as you wish, allowing any impression to fill your awareness, then gently open your eyes; with a breath, allow the chakras in the palms of your hands to open. Take up your stones and gaze into them. Let their beauty fill your mind. Let their beauty and power mingle with yours as they become part of you and you of them. Feel the divine connection, the unity consciousness. You are part of everything and everything is part of you. There is no separation—you are simply welcoming another part of you and reopening the ancient connection that has always been there between you and the rest of the universe. Feel the flood of energy now, as the wonder of this unity becomes part of your awareness. You are irrevocably connected with the whole universe, with the Divine.

Gently now, with tenderness, bring your cupped hands into the beam of light above your head. Feel the mingling energies and allow any impressions to enter into your awareness. Feel the oneness; in this moment commit to that unity, knowing that whatever you do affects the whole of humanity, the whole of the universe, the whole of creation. Know that the love that you feel is part of everything, for everything, from everything, and that your purpose is to manifest that love in every moment of your daily life, to see every being as equal, of value and deserving of your love and respect. Feel the joy of that unity and the wonder of it all. Allow any impressions to simply float into your consciousness as you enjoy your divinity.

Stay as long as you wish, while being aware of your grounding.

When you are ready, gently but firmly be aware that you are fully in your body and allow your crown chakra to close, enclosing within it the divine love that is yours, that will nourish and sustain you, keeping you forever in love, holding you in respect for yourself and all else in the universe. Gently give thanks and replace your stones on the altar or cushion, or gently place them on your wrist.

Close down all but your root chakra, which remains open to keep you grounded. Have a drink of water. Stretch and record your impressions in your journal.

Epilogue

I hope you have had a pleasant journey and will enjoy your gemstones for years to come. Loved and respected, they will serve you well.

If you started reading this book just for fun in order to learn more about your chakra power beads, you may have found things happening that you didn't quite expect. Often this is an indication that you are ready for more of the journey.

If so, perhaps we'll meet again in another book or at another time. Should you want to know more about workshops, talks and such, you could visit my website—www.brendadavies-collection.com. See you there!

Appendix 1

❧

The Use of Crystals and Gemstones in Ancient Times

Though its existence is still challenged by some people, there is much channeled information and past-life work confirming that Atlantis was a great and advanced nation in ancient times. Crystals and gemstones were an essential part of the Atlantean culture, used for a wide variety of purposes ranging from channeling and harnessing cosmic forces to holding records and aiding telepathic communication. The natural electromagnetic energy of quartz crystal was used to store and amplify power, while priests used crystals to effect mental, physical and spiritual changes, especially in those who were mentally ill or demonstrated criminal tendencies. Cavernous crystal chambers, where color, vibration and sound increased the effectiveness, were used for healing. This practice was also later employed in Egypt, where such caverns can still be visited today. Their energy is awesome. Atlanteans also used crystals in mystical rites, to make tools and to power transport. They may also have used them to attract the radioactive energies of stellar bodies.

It is thought that volcanic eruptions divided the continent of Atlantis into a series of islands and the Atlantean people were scattered to different parts of the world, taking with them their knowledge of how to use crystals.

The Native American people tell stories of them having come to America in large boats from an island they call Atlan. They continued to use crystals for divination, much as many healers and clairvoyants do today. Flint was then used to fashion tools and weapons. The Mayan culture used crystals and gemstones for diagnosis and treatment, while the Toltecs used them in temples and initiates used crystal mirrors to train their latent visionary capacity much as we might now use a crystal ball.

In Egypt, South America and Tibet, crystals were used for a variety of purposes. For instance, in Egypt priests used golden discs bearing crystals to focus the sun's energy on parts of people's bodies to heal and restore well-being. And of course Egyptian queens such as Cleopatra used ground lapis and malachite as makeup.

Crystal skulls millions of years old have been found in various sites around the world. Some of them have been found to carry great healing powers and also to transmit ancient wisdom. The properties of some are enhanced by the addition of other crystals that fit into the eye sockets.

It is thought that rock crystal was used in the building of the great pyramids and in the erection of stone circles such as Stonehenge. The Great Pyramid at Giza is capped with alabaster, a form of gypsum. Though the Giza pyramids and the Sphinx are the subject of several theories, these structures may have been built by Atlanteans before the great flood as replicas of ancient temples of Atlantis.

Ancient astrology texts and the bible advise on the use of stones as talismans and amulets, and also contain advice on their medicinal and protective benefits. Stones have been worn to bring good luck, to protect from harm, to help women become pregnant and for a wide range of other emotional, physical and psychological problems. Though some of these practices are born of superstition and hardly based in reality, many of the minerals have properties that show strong scientific basis and are used in medicine and industry today.

Appendix 2

※

Some Technical Data

Here are some technical odds and ends you might like to know about.

Moh's Scale

This scale, designed by the Austrian mineralogist Friedrich Moh, compares the hardness and durability of gemstones alongside ten well-known substances. The durability and strength of the gemstone depends on the strength of the bonds between the atoms it is made of. On Moh's scale, the higher the number, the harder the stone, though the numbers do not indicate, for example, that fluorite is four times harder than talc or that quartz is seven times harder. Each of the stones can be scratched or damaged by the ones with higher a number on the scale. Knowing the position on the scale is useful since it helps us prevent damage to our precious stones. The softer ones, which are lower on the scale, need to be stored separately. Calcite, for instance, is best laid on some cotton in a box where it will usually stay, or placed under glass.

1. Talc

2. Gypsum

3. Calcite

4. Fluorite

5. Apatite (can be used for the solar plexus)

6. Feldspar—labradorite, moonstone, sunstone

7. Quartz—all of the quartz group—amethyst, citrine, smoky quartz, rose quartz, ametrine, aventurine, jasper, agate, carnelian, tiger's eye, calcedony, chrysoprase, onyx, sardonyx

8. Topaz

9. Corundum—sapphire

10. Diamond (this is the hardest material known)

Crystal Systems

There are seven crystalline structures that help classify gemstones:

Cubic (e.g., diamond, garnet, fluorite, magnetite)

Hexagonal (e.g., emerald, aquamarine, apatite, beryl, morganite)

Tetragonal (e.g., zircon, rutile)

Trigonal (e.g., quartz, sapphire, calcite, rhodochrosite)

Triclinic (e.g., turquoise, sunstone, labradorite)

Orthorhombic (e.g., peridot, topaz)

Monoclinic (e.g., moonstone, jadeite, azurite, kunzite, malachite)

As always, there are exceptions to any rule, and in the case of crystals some take on no particular structure—the amorphous gemstones. These include obsidian and moldavite.

Bibliography

Bunn, Charles. *Crystals—Their Role in Nature and Science*. Academic Press, 1964.

Burgess, Jaquie. *Crystals for Life*. Newleaf, 2000.

Chocron, Daya Sarai. *Healing with Crystals and Gemstones*. Samuel Weiser, 1986.

Davies, Dr. Brenda. *The 7 Healing Chakras*. Ulysses Press, 2000.

———*Unlocking the Heart Chakra*. Ulysses Press, 2001.

Davies, Dr. Brenda, & Jones, Dr. Hilary. *Total Wellbeing*. Hodder & Stoughton, 1999.

Gienger, Michael. *Crystal Power, Crystal Healing—The Complete Handbook*. Blandford, 1998.

Glade, Phyllis. *Crystal Healing—The Next Step*. Llewelyn Publications, 1993.

Harold, Edmund. *Crystal Healing*. Aquarian Press, 1986.

Harrison, Stephanie and Tim. *Crystal Therapy*. Element 2000.

———*Crystal Therapy—An Introductory Guide to Crystals for Health and Well-being*. Element, 2000.

Melody. *Love in the Earth: A Kaleidoscope of Crystals*. Earth-Love Publishing House, 1995.

Roeder, Dorothy. *Crystal Co-Creators*. Light Technology Publishing, 1994.

Silbey, Uma. *The Complete Crystal Guidebook*. Bantam New Age, 1986.

Simpson, Liz. *The Book of Crystal Healing*. Gaia Books, 1997.

Raphaell, Katrina. *Crystal Enlightenment: The Transforming Properties of Crystals and Healing Stones*. Aurora Press, 1985.

Schumann, Walter. *Gemstones of the World*. N.A.G. Press, 1977.

Walters, Raymond J. L. *The Healing Power of Gemstones*. Carlton, 2000.

Other Ulysses Press Mind/Body Titles

GIVE YOUR FACE A LIFT:
NATURAL WAYS TO LOOK AND FEEL GOOD
Penny Stanway, $17.95
This full-color guide to natural face care tells how to give oneself a "natural facelift" using oils, creams, masks and homemade products that nourish and beautify the skin.

HERBS THAT WORK:
THE SCIENTIFIC EVIDENCE OF THEIR HEALING POWERS
David Armstrong, $12.95
Unlike herb books relying on folklore or vague anecdotes, *Herbs that Work* is the first consumer guide to rate herbal remedies based on documented, state-of-the-art scientific research.

HOW TO MEDITATE: AN ILLUSTRATED GUIDE
TO CALMING THE MIND AND RELAXING THE BODY
Paul Roland, $16.95
Offers a friendly, illustrated approach to calming the mind and raising consciousness through various techniques, including basic meditation, visualization, body scanning for tension, affirmations and mantras.

HOW MEDITATION HEALS: A SCIENTIFIC EXPLANATION
Eric Harrison, $12.95
In straightforward, practical terms, this book details the proven health benefits of meditation and reveals how and why meditation improves the natural functioning of the human body.

THE JOSEPH H. PILATES METHOD AT HOME:
A BALANCE, SHAPE, STRENGTH & FITNESS PROGRAM
Eleanor McKenzie, $16.95
This handbook describes and details Pilates, a mental and physical program that combines elements of yoga and classical dance.

KNOW YOUR BODY: THE ATLAS OF ANATOMY
2nd edition, Introduction by Emmet B. Keeffe, M.D., $14.95
Provides a comprehensive, full-color guide to the human body.

101 SIMPLE WAYS TO MAKE YOUR HOME & FAMILY
SAFE IN A TOXIC WORLD
Beth Ann Petro Roybal, $9.95
Sheds light on common toxins found around the house and offers parents straightforward ways to protect themselves and their children.

PILATES WORKBOOK: ILLUSTRATED STEP-BY-STEP GUIDE
TO MATWORK TECHNIQUES
Michael King, $12.95
Illustrates the core matwork movements exactly as Joseph Pilates
intended them to be performed; readers learn each movement by simply
following the photographic sequences and explanatory captions.

SENSES WIDE OPEN:
THE ART AND PRACTICE OF LIVING IN YOUR BODY
Johanna Putnoi, $14.95
Through simple, accessible exercises, this book shows how to be
at ease with yourself and experience genuine pleasure in your
physical connection to others and the world.

THE 7 HEALING CHAKRAS:
UNLOCKING YOUR BODY'S ENERGY CENTERS
Brenda Davies, $14.95
Explores the essence of chakras, vortices of energy that connect the
physical body with the spiritual.

SIMPLY RELAX:
AN ILLUSTRATED GUIDE TO SLOWING DOWN AND ENJOYING LIFE
Dr. Sarah Brewer, $15.95
In a beautifully illustrated format, this book clearly presents physical
and mental disciplines that show readers how to relax.

TEACH YOURSELF TO MEDITATE IN 10 SIMPLE LESSONS: DISCOVER
RELAXATION AND CLARITY OF MIND IN JUST MINUTES A DAY
Eric Harrison, $12.95
Guides the reader through ten easy-to-follow core meditations. Also
included are practical and enjoyable "spot meditations" that require
only a few minutes a day and can be incorporated into the busiest of
schedules.

UNLOCKING THE HEART CHAKRA:
HEAL YOUR RELATIONSHIPS WITH LOVE
Brenda Davies, $14.95
Applying the principles of the chakra system, *Unlocking the Heart Chakra*
examines the central relationships in our lives and offers a plan for
understanding them.

*To order these books call 800-377-2542 or 510-601-8301, fax 510-601-8307, e-mail
ulysses@ulyssespress.com, or write to Ulysses Press, P.O. Box 3440, Berkeley, CA
94703. All retail orders are shipped free of charge. California residents must include
sales tax. Allow two to three weeks for delivery.*

About the Author

Dr. Brenda Davies, a British psychiatrist and spiritual healer, combines her traditional medical training with ancient healing gifts. Having lived and worked around the world, she now resides in Texas, though her workshops, clients and conferences keep her on an international circuit. A mother of two and grandmother of one, she is happily living her own spiritual path while exploring the frontiers of love and healing.

Chakra Power Bead Bracelet Offer

❧

Buy one of our Chakra Power Bead bracelets and receive a second bracelet FREE* (a $10 value). Choose from:

- ❧ *Root Chakra Dark Red Power Bead Bracelet* (power)
- ❧ *Sacral Chakra Orange Power Bead Bracelet* (rejuvenation)
- ❧ *Solar Plexus Chakra Yellow Power Bead Bracelet* (tranquility)
- ❧ *Heart Chakra Red Power Bead Bracelet* (love)
- ❧ *Throat Chakra Light Blue Power Bead Bracelet* (health)
- ❧ *Brow Chakra Violet Power Bead Bracelet* (mental focus)
- ❧ *Crown Chakra Clear Power Bead Bracelet* (spirituality)

Our bracelets are made from quality semiprecious stones, and we guarantee your satisfaction or your money back.

* The free Chakra Power Bead bracelet is available to all buyers of this book in the United States, Canada and the United Kingdom. Please send an order (indicating which two bracelets you would like) along with US$10, your name and address to:

Chakra Power Bead Bracelet Offer
Ulysses Press
P.O. Box 3440
Berkeley, CA 94703

Or call 800-377-2542 (USA), 510-601-8301 (international).

Purchase additional bracelets for $10 each, or the complete set of 7 bracelets (6 plus your free bracelet) for only $45.